T0326295

Holding Yin, Embracing Yang

Books by Eva Wong

Cultivating Stillness
Cultivating the Energy of Life
Feng-shui
Harmonizing Yin and Yang
Holding Yin, Embracing Yang
Lieh-tzu
A Master Course in Feng-shui
Nourishing the Essence of Life
The Pocket Tao Reader
Seven Taoist Masters
The Shambhala Guide to Taoism
Tales of the Dancing Dragon: Stories of the Tao
Tales of the Taoist Immortals
Teachings of the Tao

Holding Yin, Embracing Yang

THREE TAOIST CLASSICS ON
MEDITATION, BREATH REGULATION,
SEXUAL YOGA, AND THE CIRCULATION
OF INTERNAL ENERGY

Translated with an introduction by
Eva Wong

SHAMBHALA
Boulder
2005

Shambhala Publications, Inc.
2129 13th Street
Boulder, Colorado 80302
www.shambhala.com
© 2005 by Eva Wong

Printed in the United States of America

Shambhala Publications is distributed worldwide by Penguin Random
House, Inc., and its subsidiaries.

Library of Congress Cataloging-in-Publication Data
Holding yin, embracing yang: three Taoist classics on meditation, breath
regulation, sexual yoga, and the circulation of internal
energy/ Translated with an Introduction by Eva Wong.—1st ed.
p. cm.
ISBN 978-1-59030-263-7 (pbk.: alk. paper)
1. Taoism. 2. Hygiene, Taoist. I. Wang, Eva, 1964–
BL1920.H65 2005
299.5' 148—dc22

2004024705

Contents

DISCUSSION ON THE CAVITY OF THE TAO
(Daojiaotan)

Holding Yin, Embracing Yang

Translator's Introduction

The texts in this collection were chosen to highlight the Taoist practices of meditation, breath regulation, the microcosmic and macrocosmic circulations, and sexual (consort) alchemy. The *Treatise on the Mysterious Orifice* (*Xuanweilun*) was written by Lu Xixing (1520–1606); both the *Discussion on the Cavity of the Tao* (*Daojiaotan*) and *Secret Teachings on the Three Wheels* (*Sanjubizhi*) were lectures by Li Xiyue (1806–1856) compiled by his students.

The practices of meditation, breath regulation, the microcosmic and macrocosmic circulations, and sexual yoga are methods of Taoist internal alchemy. Internal alchemy is the discipline of cultivating health, longevity, and immortality by transforming the energetic structures of body and mind. Today, there are four recognized schools of Taoist internal alchemy: the Northern, Southern, Eastern, and Western schools, named after the geographic regions of China where they originated.

THE NORTHERN SCHOOL

There are two branches of the Northern school. The first branch is the Northern Complete Reality school (Beiquanzhen), founded by Wang Chongyang; the second is the Pre-celestial Limitless sect (Xientienwujimen), founded by Chen Xiyi. Both schools originated in the Song dynasty (960–1279 C.E.); both taught that mind should be cultivated before body, and neither uses techniques of sexual alchemy. The teachings of the Northern Complete Reality school are best represented by the Dragon Gate (Longmen) sect. This monastic sect was founded by Wang Chongyang's student Qiu Changchun. The Pre-celestial Limitless sect of Chen Xiyi is a nonmonastic hermit lineage, its teachings transmitted orally from master to student. Practitioners of both branches of the Northern school are usually initiated into the lineage when they are young. (Qiu Changchun himself was a teenager when he began his spiritual training.) This probably explains why the Northern school favored techniques of the single path (practicing without the help of a consort). Since little to none of their generative energy was lost, the practitioners need not replenish their energy by gathering it from a partner. Today, there are Dragon Gate–affiliated monasteries worldwide, but the influence of Northern Complete Reality Taoism is still strongest in northern China. The influence of the Pre-celestial Limitless sect is less easy to document because of its hermit lineage, but small groups of its practitioners are found throughout mainland China, Taiwan, and Hong Kong. (More information on the teachings and practices of the Northern Complete Reality school and the Pre-celestial Limitless sect can be found in my *Shambhala Guide to Taoism, Cultivating Stillness, Cultivating the Energy of Life,* and *Nourishing the Essence of Life.*)

The Southern School

The southern branch of the Complete Reality school, the Southern school not only taught that body needs to be cultivated before mind, but also uses techniques of sexual yoga (the paired path). Although Zhang Boduan of the Song dynasty is acknowledged as the founder of this school, the division within the Complete Reality school already existed during the time of his teacher Liu Haichan. Both Liu Haichan and Wang Chongyang had studied with Lu Dongbin, the patriarch of modern Taoist internal alchemy. While Wang favored the single path, probably because of his Confucian and Chan Buddhist influences, Liu and Zhang both tended to be pragmatic and taught single or paired practice according to the needs of their students. This is probably because they both started Taoist cultivation late in life and understood how paired practice could help older students. There are several important differences between the Southern Complete Reality school and its northern counterpart. First, the southern branch is not monastic. Second, most of its practitioners tended to be householders who had raised families before studying the arts of longevity. Having lost much generative energy over the years, these practitioners needed a quick way to replenish it. Sexual alchemy, or paired practice, allowed them to do exactly that. The Southern school considered the paired path a matter of convenience, its techniques useful for replenishing generative energy in the early phases of cultivation. Once generative energy is plentiful, practitioners will switch to techniques of the single path. Third, because it is a lay tradition, the Southern school was and still is a loosely knit group of practitioners led by independent teachers. Spread over the areas south of the Yangzi River, practitioners of the Southern school follow teachers who often added "personal touches" to the teachings. Eventually, some of these personal touches evolved into distinct lineages. One was the Eastern school of Lu Xixing, and the other was the Western school of Li Xiyue.

(More information on the teachings of the Southern Complete Reality school can be found in my *Nourishing the Essence of Life*.)

THE EASTERN SCHOOL

Lu Xixing, also known as Lu Qianxui, is the founder of the Eastern school. His unique teachings on combining the single and paired paths attracted a large number of students in southeast China, especially in his home province of Jiangsu. Since most of his followers lived in eastern China, his teachings are named the Eastern school. Lu began his career as a Confucian scholar. After several unsuccessful attempts at passing the civil examinations, he embraced Taoism. Initially, he was attracted to the teachings of the Northern Complete Reality school. However, after meeting Taoist teachers who taught him the methods of sexual alchemy, he realized that the two approaches (single and paired practice) were not necessarily contradictory. His own experimentation with the two practices led him to devise an approach that combined the best of both. In later years, he also incorporated Chan (Zen) meditation into his practice. It is probably because of Lu's early interest in Northern Complete Reality Taoism and later interest in Chan Buddhism that sexual alchemy was regarded as a secondary practice for the Eastern school. Paired practice was recommended only for older and weaker students so they could quickly build the foundations necessary for the higher levels of internal alchemy. Regardless of their age, once practitioners reached intermediate levels of internal development, single cultivation was the preferred practice.

Lu Xixing wrote prolifically. His writings include commentaries on the *Zhuangzi,* Zhang Boduan's classic *Understanding Reality (Wuzhenpian)*, original treatises on combined single and paired practice, as well as guides to reading the *Avatamsaka Sutra*.

THE WESTERN SCHOOL

Li Xiyue, known as Li Hanxui and Duanyangzi, is the founder of the Western school. Like Lu Xixing, Li was adept at both the single and paired paths. However, Li's cultural and spiritual background is radically different from Lu's. First, Li Xiyue was never a Confucian and never aspired to become a government official. Second, although he respected Buddhism, Li never developed an interest in Chan meditation. Finally, whereas Lu traveled extensively throughout China and tended to be cosmopolitan in outlook, Li was very much a product of his native Sichuan culture. Sichuan is one of the most insular regions of China. Situated in a river basin surrounded by mountains and accessible only through the Yangzi River gorge, Sichuan developed a unique cultural heritage. Typically distrustful of mainstream Chinese culture and fiercely loyal to local customs, Sichuan natives take pride in both preserving and propagating their uniqueness. Historically, it has been said that if mainstream Chinese culture entered Sichuan, it would not assimilate Sichuan but be assimilated instead. It is against this background of Sichuan culture that the teachings of Li Xiyue should be understood.

According to the lineage chronicles of the Western school, Zhang Boduan, the founder of the Southern Complete Reality school, received the teachings of paired practice from a hermit in Sichuan. The hermit himself was said to have studied with Liu Haichan, who in turn had received the teachings from Lu Dongbin himself. And from whom did Lu Dongbin receive the teachings of paired practice? According to the Western school, Lu learned the techniques of sexual alchemy from a hermit while wandering in the Omei Mountains in Sichuan. Thus, the followers of the Western school considered themselves the direct spiritual successors of Lu Dongbin's teachings on sexual alchemy. Adding a touch of regional pride, they alleged that Lu himself had learned paired practice from a Sichuan native.

We can't know whether Lu Dongbin indeed learned sexual alchemy from a hermit in Sichuan, for there are no records other than those of the Western school. However, independent sources tell us that Li Xiyue studied the teachings of Lu Xixing and wrote commentaries on Lu's writings as well as editing them. That Li Xiyue was influenced by the teachings of the Eastern school was beyond doubt, but Li's approach to paired practice is different from Lu's. First, Lu Xixing viewed paired practice as a viable technique for those who begin their cultivation late in life. For Li, however, paired practice was not merely viable but preferred. Second, for the Eastern school, paired practice is used only in the early stages of internal alchemy for replenishing generative energy. Once practitioners have attained a sufficient level of generative energy, single practice was the preferred path. For the Western school, however, the paired path is practiced beyond the initial stage of building the foundations, so that today the practices of the Western school are synonymous with sexual alchemy.

The teachings of the Eastern and Western schools, especially the theory and practice of the paired path, are not easy to understand even for those who are familiar with Taoist internal alchemy. What follows is an introduction to some key concepts that are central to understanding the three texts. Keep in mind that no one school is the sole authority on Taoist spiritual practices. Moreover, each school defines the alchemical terms differently, and a text should be read within the context of the teachings of that school.

Original Nature and Primordial Life Energy

We owe our lives to the primordial life-giving and life-nourishing energy of the Tao. This energy enters our mother's womb when we are conceived and is no different from the energy that gives life to and nourishes all things.

When we are born, this primordial energy is first manifested as original nature (original mind) and life energy. The energy of original mind travels to the upper *dantien* (the area between the two eyes), and the primordial life energy travels to the kidneys. The goal of Taoist practice is to return these two energies to their primordial state and unite them. To this end, original mind is used to refine and cultivate life energy, and life energy is used to refine and cultivate original mind. When the duality of original mind and life energy dissolves, the undifferentiated primordial energy of the Tao will emerge within.

The Three Treasures

The primordial energy is also manifested as spirit, vital, and generative energies. These energies are called the three treasures because they embody the essence of life. If we preserve them, we will live; if we squander them, we will die. The primordial qualities of these energies are strong in infants. However, with growth, puberty, and maturity, these energies become contaminated. Pristine vital energy is contaminated by mundane air with each breath we take; pristine spirit energy is degraded with increasing thoughts and conceptions; and pristine generative energy leaks out of the body as procreative energy at puberty. Not knowing how to conserve these life-nourishing energies, we squander the three treasures, and we age and die before our time. The goal of Taoist practice is to preserve, cultivate, and refine these energies so that we can attain an indestructible body and enlightened mind.

Three Paths of Cultivating Body and Mind

There are three paths of cultivating body and mind in Taoist spirituality: the celestial, the terrestrial, and the human.

The celestial path is the ideal path; it is short, straightforward, and easy. In this path, internal energies are gathered and cultivated while they are pristine. Therefore, it is most optimal for people who begin their cultivation before puberty. The celestial path is also called the single path because generative, vital, and spirit energies are cultivated without help from a sexual partner.

The terrestrial path is involved with ingesting minerals and using them to transform and refine internal energy. This path requires timely application of the minerals at each stage of internal alchemical transformation. Incorrect usage of minerals can lead to poisoning and death.

The human path is associated with paired practice. In this path, energy is gathered from a partner to replenish generative energy that was lost. The Eastern and Western schools recommend this path for practitioners who start cultivation late in life. The more quickly generative energy can be replenished, the sooner the practitioner can advance to the higher stages of internal alchemy. The human path of cultivating body and mind is chosen for convenience when the celestial path becomes impractical.

Pre-celestial and Post-celestial

In the texts, there are four contexts in which pre- and post-celestial are used. First, pre- and post-celestial are used to describe two states of reality. Entities that do not have form, structure, or appearance are pre-celestial in nature, while entities that have these qualities are post-celestial in nature. Thus, for example, original nature, which has no form or structure, is pre-celestial, and generative energy in the form of blood or seminal fluid, which has form and appearance, is post-celestial.

Second, pre- and post-celestial are used to contrast two kinds of human existence. In this context, pre-celestial refers to the state of existence before the onset of puberty, when spirit, vital, and generative energies are primordial and pristine. In contrast, post-celestial refers to the state of existence after the onset of puberty, when the three energies have been contaminated by thoughts, feelings, and desires. Thus, for example, persons who have not lost generative energy are said to possess a pre-celestial body, and those who have lost generative energy are said to possess a post-celestial body.

Third, pre- and post-celestial are used to describe two kinds of medicines necessary for internal alchemical transformations. Pre-celestial medicines are generated from within, while post-celestial medicines are collected from outside. Thus, for example, generative energy produced by our own body is pre-celestial in nature. Original mind, which is the primordial manifestation of spirit energy, is also pre-celestial. Generative energy collected from a partner, however, is post-celestial medicine. On the other hand, generative energy that is produced within, even when it is aroused by a partner during paired practice, is considered pre-celestial.

Fourth, pre- and post-celestial are used to classify methods of internal alchemy. The single path is considered pre-celestial because it works with pre-celestial energies and because it is best suited for persons who possess a pre-celestial body. Pre-celestial practices are described as the forward path because they follow the natural way of the Tao. Paired practice is considered post-celestial because the source of energy used to replenish and stimulate a practitioner's generative energy is from outside his or her own body. The paired path is optimal for persons who no longer possess a pre-celestial body. Post-celestial practices follow the path of reversal because they work with absorbing external energy and directing it from the outside to the inside.

Single Practice and Paired Practice

Single practice, or the single path, requires the practitioner to cultivate alone. Paired practice, or the paired path, involves the joint action of the practitioner and the partner. Paired practice is also called sexual alchemy or sexual yoga because the practitioner receives help from a consort to replenish his or her generative energy. In a nutshell, paired practice is concerned with recovering energy that was lost, and single practice is concerned with cultivating energy that is already there.

Single practice is best suited for persons who begin cultivation before generative energy has been aroused and used for procreation or pleasure. When generative energy is plentiful, the practitioner needs only to cultivate clarity and stillness of mind in order for generative energy to be transmuted into vital energy, and vital energy to be transmuted into spirit energy. The paired path, on the other hand, is more practical for persons beginning cultivation late in life. When generative energy is insufficient, it cannot be transmuted into vital energy and spirit energy. The methods of the paired path are designed to help practitioners build up their reservoir of generative energy by obtaining it from an external source.

In Taoist sexual alchemy, paired practice is a method of convenience, used only when single practice is deemed ineffective. The texts in this collection describe single practice as the path of high virtue and paired practice as the path of low virtue. This should not be taken to mean that practitioners of the single path are more virtuous or ethical than practitioners of the paired path. In this context, high virtue refers to pre-celestial existence and low virtue to post-celestial existence. The path of high virtue is called the celestial path because it is closer to the natural way of the Tao. In contrast, the path of low virtue is called the human path because it is farther removed from the Tao. This logic is derived from a statement from the *Tao Te Ching*: "Humanity follows the way of heaven; heaven follows the way of the Tao; and the Tao follows its own natural way."

A practical concern for older practitioners is that they do not have much time in their lives to accumulate and transmute generative energy naturally. Practiced properly, sexual alchemy can help them strengthen generative energy by collecting it from a partner. Generative energy is strengthened through paired practice in two stages. First, by gathering generative energy from a partner, practitioners can replenish and build up a store of energy. Second, once a sufficient level of generative energy is stored within, paired practice can stimulate the arousal and emergence of the practitioner's own internal generative energy. In this latter method, the consort helps the practitioner to arouse the production of generative energy rather than supplying it. Needless to say, the practitioner must possess the discipline to turn the flow of the aroused energy back into the body and not eject it out of the body.

For paired practice to work properly, the practitioner must cultivate clarity and stillness of mind. Taoist sexual yoga is not equivalent to bedchamber techniques designed to conserve generative energy. Also, contrary to some popular opinions, it is not about improving sexual enjoyment or strengthening the sexual bond between partners. Unless the practitioner empties the mind and dissolves desire, paired practice can be harmful. All three texts stress the necessity of stilling the mind as a prerequisite for practicing sexual alchemy.

Paired practice also requires tremendous discipline from both the practitioner and the consort. If desire arises during the gathering or arousing of sexual energy, the internal energy of the practitioner will be drained. The consort must be trained to work with the practitioner and be attuned to the partner's flow and ebb of energy. Contrary to what some have argued, Taoist sexual yoga does not exploit the consort. With proper training, the consort is a willing partner whose energy is replenished, not drained, while assisting the practitioner.

While the texts in this collection do not discuss who can be a consort, contemporary practitioners of sexual alchemy acknowledge that the consort can be male or female. Thus, not only can male practitioners be aided by a female consort (as is generally believed), but female practitioners can be aided by a male consort, and both male and female practitioners can be aided by a consort of their own sex. Used properly, sexual alchemy is an example of how mind is used to cultivate body and body is used to cultivate mind.

STAGES IN THE ALCHEMY OF INTERNAL TRANSFORMATION

There are four stages of internal transformation: transmuting generative energy into vital energy, transmuting vital energy into spirit energy, refining the spirit to return to the void, and refining the void to merge with the Tao.

Single-path practitioners start with the transmutation of generative energy into vital energy by gathering generative essence produced naturally in the body at the hour of *zi* (11 P.M.–1 A.M.). Paired-path practitioners begin by gathering energy from a partner. When sufficient energy is gathered, generative energy can be transmuted into vital energy. When there is a sufficient store of vital energy (or vapor), the three gates of the *du* meridian along the spinal column will open, and the Microcosmic Orbit (the waterwheel) can be engaged. This waterwheel is referred to as the first waterwheel. It circulates vapor and is sometimes called the firewheel, because internal heat is used to drive the vapor through the circuit.

The next stage of alchemical transformation involves the transmutation of vital energy into spirit energy. The goal of this stage is to conceive the sacred fetus, which is the seed of the primordial spirit *(yuanshen)*. In this stage, mind is refined, original nature of emptiness is recovered, and body is continuously nourished by the circulation of vapor. Central to this stage of alchemical transformation is the production of the golden and jade elixirs. The golden elixir is essential to nourishing the body, and it is attained by taming the mind and dissolving desire. The jade elixir is essential to refining the mind, and it is attained by arousing generative essence and transmuting it into vapor. Thus, the elixir that emerges from cultivating the mind is used to nourish the body, and the elixir that emerges from cultivating the body is used to temper the mind. Single-path practitioners attain both the golden and jade elixirs by cultivating clarity and stillness. In the paired path, the teachings of the Eastern and Western schools diverge. In the Eastern school, paired practice ends, and practitioners follow the single path of cultivation from here on. The Western school, however, continues to use sexual alchemy to stimulate the production of generative essence for the transmutation of generative energy into vital energy.

The circulation of the jade elixir and its return to the dantien are the work of the second waterwheel. This circulation generates a sensation of coolness, because the substance circulated is generative essence, which is watery in nature. The work of the second waterwheel is referred to as the lesser return, or the return of the numeric seven to the lower dantien. When sufficient vapor is accumulated and transmuted into spirit energy, the immortal fetus, or *yuanshen*, will be conceived. This bundle of energy settles in the lower dantien and is continuously nourished by vapor transported through the Microcosmic Orbit.

The next stage of alchemical transformation involves refining the spirit and returning it to the void. In this stage, the fetus is incubated and nourished by the golden and jade elixirs. The two elixirs originate in the lower dantien. From there, they are circulated through the du and ren meridians and then returned to where they originated. The process of returning the golden elixir to the dantien is called the greater return, or the return of the numeric nine to the dantien. This circulation is the work of the third waterwheel, called the Great Waterwheel or the Macrocosmic Orbit. This stage of internal transformation is called "refining the spirit to return to the void" because emptiness, clarity, and stillness of mind are required for engaging the Macrocosmic Orbit. From here on, all practitioners follow the single path. All alchemical transformations now occur within: Generative energy is produced and transmuted naturally, flowing and ebbing with its natural cycle; the Great Waterwheel runs naturally and smoothly; and the mind is naturally clear and still.

The final stage of alchemical transmutation is refining the void to merge with the Tao. In this stage, the practitioner abides in absolute stillness as the primordial spirit *(yuanshen)* exits the body and returns freely. Externally, the golden elixir bathes the body with a golden aura, protecting the bodily shell while the spirit travels to learn the path of the return to the Tao. Internally, the jade elixir circulates endlessly to keep the body healthy and strong. When the appropriate time comes, the spirit will leave its shell permanently and make its final journey to merge with the Tao, to be one with the primordial energy that it originally came from.

MEDITATION AND THE CULTIVATION OF CLARITY AND STILLNESS

Meditation and the cultivation of clarity and stillness are integral to both single and paired practice. The internal alchemical transformations will not occur—or, worse, could go wrong—if the practitioner does not clear the mind of thoughts and desires.

Meditation is essential at all stages of internal alchemy. Initially, meditation serves to quiet the mind, relax the body, and familiarize the practitioner with postures that will be important in the later stages of training. In single practice, the cultivation of stillness, clarity, and emptiness is the key to the entire path. In fact, the single path is referred to as the path of clarity and stillness. Practitioners on this path will attain the internal transformations naturally if they are able to cultivate stillness. In paired practice, meditation is used to dissolve desire and empty the mind in order for sexual alchemy to work. If desire is present when a practitioner is gathering generative energy from a partner or when the partner is helping the practitioner to stimulate the production of generative energy from within, the practitioner's own energy will leak out. This is why sexual alchemy is useless or even dangerous if mind is not tamed in the early stage of building the foundations.

In the transmutation of vital energy to spirit energy, the cultivation of clarity and stillness is necessary for refining and circulating internal energy. It is only in stillness that the fire will be ignited and heat will travel through the Microcosmic Orbit. The conception of the immortal fetus also requires the practitioner to gather vapor by focusing the spirit, and focusing the spirit requires emptying the mind and dissolving the dualities of outside and inside, thinker and thoughts, and actor and actions.

In refining the spirit to return to the void, the spirit, in the form of the immortal fetus, is nourished and brought to maturity. To focus the spirit is to gather the spirit into the One cavity, and the One cavity emerges only when the mind is in absolute stillness. While carrying the fetus, the body must be nourished continuously by the jade and golden elixirs, and for these elixirs to circulate, the mind must be empty and still. If the bodily shell is not nourished by the elixirs, the spirit can weaken and perish.

In refining the void to return to the Tao, there is only one practice: abiding in absolute stillness while the spirit exits and returns to the body. It is no coincidence that the alchemical classics describe this stage as "nine years of facing the wall."

BREATH REGULATION

Breath regulation is central to Taoist internal alchemy. Taoist practice distinguishes two kinds of breath: mundane breath and true breath. The breath of the typical person is mundane breath, which is described as shallow because it involves breathing through the nostrils or the mouth. The breath of the seasoned practitioner is described as heavy because it involves breathing with the belly, specifically the lower dantien.

Taoist spiritual practice works with both mundane and true breath. By focusing on the inhalation and exhalation of mundane breath, the mind can be drawn away from objects in the external world, and by consciously slowing the cycle of inhalation and exhalation during meditation, both body and mind can relax and enter stillness. When the practitioner no longer needs to focus on inhalation and exhalation in order to still the mind, mundane breath will cease and true breath will emerge.

True breath originates in the navel and is subtle and deep. The functions of true breath are many. First, it is used to transport vapor and generative energy through the Microcosmic Orbit to nourish the body. Second, it is used to regulate the internal fire to transmute generative energy into vital energy, burn the residues of ego from the mind, and incubate the immortal fetus. Third, it is used to circulate the jade and golden elixirs in the Macrocosmic Orbit to refine the body and nourish the immortal fetus. Finally, the true breath is the liaison between spirit, vapor, and generative essence. Spirit itself is still. However, when merged with the true breath, spirit can be circulated with vapor and generative essence, thus uniting the three treasures in movement.

Breath regulation in the higher levels of Taoist internal alchemy is natural and not controlled by mind. The entire body is involved in inhalation and exhalation, and during each cycle of breath, the body absorbs the primordial energy of the universe and uses it to renew the body. The transformations of body and mind cannot occur without the true breath, and the true breath will not emerge if the mind is not empty and spirit is not focused.

THE WATERWHEEL (MICROCOSMIC AND MACROCOSMIC ORBITS)

The waterwheel is a circuit or conduit that transports internal energy. This conduit is made up of two meridians: du and ren. Along each meridian are critical points where major internal alchemical work occurs (see figures 1 and 2). The du meridian runs from the base of the spine to the top of the head and down to the mouth. At the palate, it joins the ren meridian, which runs down the front of the body and circles back to the base of the spine. The text *Secret Teachings on the Three Wheels* describes three waterwheels, each with a different function in the alchemy of internal transformation. The first waterwheel is used to circulate vapor; the sensation of its movement is associated with heat. The second wheel circulates generative essence; the sensation of its movement is described as electrical. These two waterwheels are known as the Microcosmic Orbit. The third waterwheel is involved with returning the jade and golden elixirs (the numerics seven and nine) to the lower dantien. This is the Macrocosmic Orbit, and its sensation is associated with coolness.

The waterwheel is described as a circuit because, like an electrical circuit, energy will flow through it when it is open. The circuit is called the waterwheel because it transports substances that are watery in nature: vapor, generative essence, and the two elixirs.

There are several systems of movement in the waterwheel. Initially, the motion of the waterwheel is direction-specific: up the spine and down the front of the body. Upward movement is concerned with the transmutation of generative energy into vital energy and vital energy into spirit energy; and downward movement is concerned with the creation of vital energy by spirit energy and the creation of generative energy by vital energy. With time and practice, the circulation becomes smooth, and the movement can go up the front of the body and down the spine as well. Eventually, the transportation system in the orbit becomes even more efficient, so that the two paths of circulation described above occur simultaneously.

True movement of the waterwheel is natural. Visualizing or imagining its movement will not cause it to move. Two conditions must be met before the waterwheel will turn. First, the three gates along the du meridian must be open. To open these gates, generative energy must be plentiful. When generative energy is plentiful, it can be transmuted into vapor. When there is sufficient vapor, the vapor can thrust through the du meridian and open the three gates. Second, the mind must be still and empty of thoughts. It is when stillness has reached its height that movement will begin.

The waterwheel is central to Taoist cultivation. No alchemical transformation can occur without the waterwheel. However, the work of the waterwheel does not encompass the entire process of internal alchemy. The waterwheel is a method by which the three treasures—generative, vital, and spirit energies—can be transmuted, nourished, and refined so that the practitioner can attain the indestructible body and enlightened mind and return to the Tao.

The texts in this collection contain the highest teachings of the Eastern and Western schools of Taoist internal alchemy. These texts are meant to introduce you to methods of Taoist internal practices and should not be treated as manuals. If you are interested in learning the techniques of the Eastern and Western schools, you need to find the right teachers. Following are some guidelines to help you choose a qualified teacher of either of these two schools:

First, a teacher should be knowledgeable about the theory and methods of the practices. The texts in this book are definitive classics of the Eastern and Western schools. Anyone claiming to be a teacher of these schools should be familiar with the ideas presented in the texts. Having some knowledge of the teachings from primary sources (such as translations) will help you to determine whether the instruction offered is consistent with what is taught traditionally.

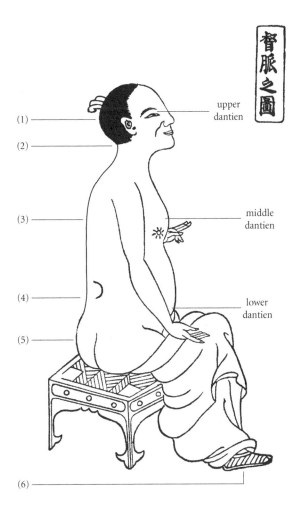

(1)
(2)
(3)
(4)
(5)
(6)

upper dantien

middle dantien

lower dantien

Figure 1

The du meridian, showing major points of internal alchemical activity mentioned in the three texts. (1) Wind House cavity. (2) Celestial Gate, also known as Jade Pillow and Upper Gate. (3) Cavity of Between the Shoulder Blades, also known as the Middle Gate. (4) Life Gate, also known as the Lower Gate. (5) Tailbone cavity. (6) Bubbling Spring. This cavity is not part of the du and ren meridians. It is mentioned in the text and shown here as reference.

Note also that the three elixir fields (upper, middle, and lower dantiens) are also shown for reference. The three elixirs are not "points" like the cavities but are regions that can encompass several cavities.

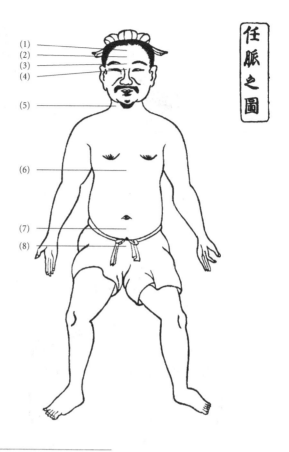

Figure 2

The ren meridian, showing major points of internal alchemical activity mentioned in the three texts. (1) Mudball cavity, also known as Celestial Valley. (2) Upper Sea of Vapor. (3) Mysterious Gate, also known as Mysterious Orifice, Celestial Wheel, Mysterious House, and Mysterious Closure. (4) Raven Bridge. (5) Pagoda. (6) Crimson Valley, also known as Middle Valley, Yellow Pavilion, and Central Palace. (7) Primal Gate, also known as Spirit Valley and Purple Pavilion. (8) Sea of Vapor, also known as Gate of the Origin, Numinous Valley, Celestial Root, Stem of Life, Cavity of Returning to the Root, and Gate of Recovering Life.

According to the texts in this collection, the Radiant Pool is located in the area between the nostrils. Other major alchemical texts locate the Radiant Pool just above the Yellow Pavilion. To avoid confusion, the Radiant Pool cavity is omitted in the figure.

Second, the notion of lineage is central to the transmission of a spiritual tradition. A lineage is a line of transmission of teachings from teacher to student. While not foolproof, lineage-based transmission is still the best way to protect against disseminating information incorrectly and inappropriately. A teacher can always identify the lineage that he or she has inherited, as well as give an account of the history of the lineage. It is not disrespectful to ask someone about their lineage. On the contrary, practitioners of lineage-based spiritual traditions will be delighted to discuss their lineage with you. I have provided sufficient information in the introduction for you to determine whether someone is a member of the lineages of these schools.

Third, a teacher will inform the prospective student of the benefits, possible dangers, and the kind of discipline demanded by the spiritual path. The practices of the Eastern and Western schools require close supervision and a lifetime of commitment. If the training program sounds too easy to be true, then it is probably not credible.

While these criteria are by no means exhaustive, they should help you find a teacher of the Eastern or Western schools of Taoist internal alchemy.

Treatise on the Mysterious Orifice

(XUANWEILUN)

I

The Three Primal Elixirs

My teachers told me that there are three primal elixirs and that these elixirs can nourish and preserve life. The three elixirs are: the primal celestial elixir, the primal terrestrial elixir, and the primal human elixir.

The primal celestial elixir is known as the sacred elixir. This elixir emerges in the sacred chamber when water rises and fire sinks. During this process, a most wondrous substance will materialize out of nothingness, and when the elixir has undergone nine circulations, it will be transformed into white snow. Refine it for two years, and you will attain the sacred talisman. If you ingest this refined elixir, your body will feel light and unencumbered. This feeling of lightness is a sign that the sacred and wondrous medicine has emerged. The primal celestial elixir can be attained by practicing the dragon-tiger technique as taught by the Yellow Emperor. The immortal Xingyang called this elixir the "elixir grains."

The primal terrestrial elixir is known as the numinous elixir. This elixir is refined from the essences of the royal minerals. Distilled from substances that have form—silver, lead, cinnabar, and mercury—this elixir can cure illnesses but cannot make the body weightless. After the elixir has circulated nine times, it will become the numinous medicine and can be used to build the sacred chamber. Because this elixir can help us return to celestial primordial existence, it has been cultivated by many practitioners. In fact, countless immortals and sages in ancient times have followed this easy and simple method of gathering pre-celestial lead to tame post-celestial mercury. However, to attain the primal terrestrial elixir, you must understand the principles of flow and ebb and know how to discriminate between the old and the youthful sprouts.

Today, there are many self-proclaimed teachers who don't understand the nature of the primal terrestrial elixir and the methods of cultivating it. As a result, their students fail to attain this elixir no matter how hard they practice. These false teachers don't know that the methods of cultivating the two kinds of elixirs described above are different. Worse, they don't realize that even talking about these methods requires knowledge of the workings of yin and yang as well as a deep understanding of the process of creation.

The primal human elixir is known as the great elixir. To realize this elixir, you need to erect the cauldron outside and refine the medicine inside. *Kan* (as symbolized by the trigram ☵) must be used to fill *li* (as symbolized by the trigram ☲). The process must occur stealthily, and the flow of the elixir must be reversed at the appropriate time. Many immortals who used this method to cultivate life received help from intimate partners.

The teachings of the three elixirs are not transmitted casually. Even the spirit-beings of the celestial and terrestrial realms are not expected to know them. The path of cultivating the celestial primal elixir is open, systematic, and bright. To walk this path, you must possess great wisdom and be favored by destiny and karma. If you meet the requirements, this approach is easy, effortless, and uncomplicated. The path of cultivating the terrestrial primal elixir is more complex. First, you must be able to hold the universe in your hands, apply the principles of internal transformation, and give birth to a body within your body. Second, you must hide your actions from ghosts and spirit-beings. Even the way in which you manipulate the workings of yin and yang must be elusive and unpredictable. The path of cultivating the primal human elixir requires the most work, and its effects will vary among practitioners. I have heard that at the highest level, this path can connect human primordial existence to terrestrial primordial existence, and eventually primordial terrestrial existence to celestial primordial existence. These then are the three primal elixirs and their properties.

2

Internal and External Medicines

In the production of the primal human elixir, the cauldron is erected outside and the medicine is refined inside. This is why we need to distinguish between the internal and external medicines. Many talk about the external medicine but know nothing about its nature or how to use it. What a pity! They are like the blind leading the blind.

The Tao is inside our bodies. So are the ingredients of the internal medicine. If the ingredients are within, why do we need to erect the cauldron outside? The ancient sages built the external cauldron only when they had no alternatives. They likened it to the use of armed force. Armed force is not desirable under normal circumstances; it is used only when there is no choice.

There are three exquisite medicines: spirit energy *(shen)*, vital energy *(qi)*, and generative energy *(jing)*. If procreative energy has never leaked out, the pre-celestial primordial energy will still be secure within. This means that there will be no need to gather energy from another source. If virginity is intact, the body will possess the qualities of the sacred fetus. However, if sexual feelings and desire have been aroused, procreative energy will be weak. Under this circumstance, we will need to strengthen it by gathering energy from an external source.

Anything that is post-celestial is yin in nature and will not last long. Therefore, if you have fallen into post-celestial existence, you will need to gather the pre-celestial equivalent of the post-celestial procreative substance to recover what you have lost. This pre-celestial substance is none other than the great yang of the metal of *qian* (sky). Only this metal can help you to refine the yin and prolong your life.

The *Triplex Unity (Zhouyicantongqi)* states: "If you want to attain immortality by ingesting substances, you must look for a substance similar to the one you possess." To put it bluntly, if a bamboo fence is broken, you must use bamboo strips to mend it, and if you want more eggs, you'll need to raise more chickens. The energy within us is no different from the energy embodied in the Great Ultimate *(taiji)*. Hidden within the Great Ultimate are the essences of yin and yang. If you are unable to follow the path of single practice, or if you don't know how to compound the minerals and ingest them, then you'll have to understand the ramifications of "the Tao being composed of one yin and one yang." Just as sounds with similar frequencies resonate with each other, energies of a similar nature will gravitate toward each other. The *Triplex Unity* also tells us: "When the energies copulate and are married to one another, the young sprouts will shoot up within a year." Understand these natural laws of creation: Human procreation is the way of mortals, and it follows the principle of forward movement; the creation of the elixir is the way of immortals, and it follows the principle of reverse movement. The natural way of the Tao is subtle and wondrous. Don't slander or belittle it. If you are able to erect the cauldron outside and refine the medicine inside, you will be able to repair your body and recover the treasures you've lost.

3

Yin and Yang Are Embedded in Each Other

What does it mean that the essences of yin and yang are hidden in their opposites? The *Triplex Unity* tells us: "Sky and earth position themselves, and the process of change works within them." By change, we mean internal transformations involving li (fire) and kan (water). In *Understanding Reality* it is stated: "First put qian (sky) and kun (earth) in the cauldron; then gather the medicines of the raven and rabbit and steam them." Qian and kun are the manifestations of yang and yin, and the raven and rabbit are their respective essences. Li is the sun, and it embodies the essence of yang. However, the middle line of the trigram li is yin in nature. Because the yin (broken) line is flanked by two yang (solid) lines, the structure of li is often described as "yin hiding in the house of yang." Kan is the moon, and it embodies the essence of yin. However, the middle line of the trigram kan is yang in nature. Because the yang line is flanked by two yin lines, the structure of kan is often described as "yang hiding in the house of yin." This is what the *Triplex Unity* means by "the male of kan is the sun and the female of li is the moon." If qian and kun represent pure yang and pure yin, then li and kan represent the interaction of yin and yang.

Before feelings and sexual desire arise, the human body is filled with the essences of pure yin and pure yang. With the arousal of sexual desire, yin and yang copulate, and the essence of generative energy is used up. The numeric associated with the young male is eight. The male reaches puberty when the numeric eight is multiplied by the numeric two (to make sixteen). The numeric associated with the young woman is seven. The female reaches puberty when the numeric seven is multiplied by two (to make fourteen). Thus, male sexual energy begins to stir and dissipate at age sixteen, and female sexual energy begins to stir and dissipate when the celestial *gui* (menstrual blood) flows out of the woman at age fourteen. This is what the texts mean by "puberty emerging when the yang numeric receives its yin complement." When the numeric of yang receives the numeric of yin, yang will become hidden in the yin. The numeric two is yin in nature. Multiply two by eight and we get sixteen. Thus, sixteen is the age when males begin to lose their generative essence. Multiply two by seven and we get fourteen. Thus, fourteen is the age when the celestial stem gui descends on the woman, and with the onset of menstruation, females begin to lose their generative energy.

The body's virginity is broken when the vapor of life is aroused, whether or not there is physical sexual contact. This is because earth pulls the heavy yin downward naturally. Each time the spark of the one yang bursts forth, a portion of life equivalent to one month is lost. Who can even begin to fathom the workings of heaven and earth? Even when sexual intercourse does not occur, the vapor of life is dissipated when generative essence is stirred. However, if we can awaken the vapor but do not excite it, we can get the generative energy to emerge in its pre-celestial and primal state. This primal generative energy is the root of all creation. Too often the vapor of life is stirred by carelessness and attachment to sights and forms. When vapor is excited, it will dissipate. When it dissipates, we will fall into the realm of post-celestial existence. This is the true meaning of breaking virginity: Virginity is broken when vapor is excited. You don't need to engage in sexual intercourse for generative energy to be drained.

When the generative essence of the male is first aroused, it is not necessarily transformed into its mundane form. It is only when vapor is transformed into fluid and fluid into semen that the pure generative essence is corrupted. When the vapor is first awakened, it is still in its pre-celestial state. However, if the pre-celestial vapor is transformed into fluid of the numeric one of water, the primal generative essence will be lost. As a result, the pre-celestial body will be broken. When vapor becomes fluid, the body will descend into post-celestial existence. With continued usage of the fluid for pleasure and procreation in the post-celestial realm, the true essence of the pre-celestial vapor will become increasingly weak. There's no reason these matters shouldn't be discussed openly. Go ask a teacher if you want to learn more.

4

Pre-celestial and Post-celestial

It is said that function and use are post-celestial in nature but the true manifestations are pre-celestial by nature. What does this mean? The true and absolute reality of pre-celestial existence cannot be seen. That which can be seen is post-celestial. Tears, saliva, semen, breath, blood, and all bodily fluids have substance and form and are therefore post-celestial in nature. Through function and use they are transformed into mundane generative, vital, and spirit energies. Many people don't know that once post-celestial existence takes over, the energies in both their post-celestial and pre-celestial forms will be lost. This is because through usage, pre-celestial existence is transformed into post-celestial existence, and in this transformation, the true nature of pre-celestial existence is lost. Sucked into the mire, the pre-celestial energies are now weak and corrupt. As a result, we age quickly, get ill easily, and die early. When the primal energies are transformed into their post-celestial form and are spent, their pre-celestial structure will not be able to endure. If you want to be strong and healthy, you must value the pre-celestial treasure within.

5

Lead and Mercury

Pre-celestial vapor is called the true lead. That which is true is the opposite of that which is mundane. What is true is formless, and what is mundane is tied to appearance. To understand the difference between the true and the mundane, you must understand the nature of reality. When qian (sky) and kun (earth) copulate, kan (water) and li (fire) are born. When qian and kun interact, the body of undifferentiated oneness is broken. This is why in the post-celestial *bagua*, qian and kun occupy unimportant positions, while the important positions (on the main axis) are given to kan and li. South and north form the limits of reality. In the pre-celestial bagua, these directions are occupied by qian and kun. In the post-celestial bagua, however, qian and kun are no longer in these locations, and the positions of power are given to kan and li. This change reflects the dominance of function and use in post-celestial existence. Li is the sun, and it shines in the south. Kan is the moon, and it shines in the north. The light of the sun and moon gives rise to all things. Although post-celestial existence is capable of giving birth, it can do so only through its connection with pre-celestial existence.

Lead is the manifestation of the true vapor of kan; it is the water that originates from the numeric one of the sky. Mercury is the manifestation of the true generative essence; it is the fire that originates from the numeric two of earth. Lead, mercury, water, and fire are names given to entities that have substance and form.

The true lead and true mercury, however, are nameless and form-less. We name them only because it is through language that we can talk about their existence. Although formless, the generative essence of yin and the vapor of yang are real. In the *Triplex Unity,* it is said that generative essence and vapor are the root substances of the universe. When these two substances merge, a human form is created. This is possible because in pre-celestial existence, each substance is embodied in the other.

The male's generative essence becomes seminal fluid with sexual arousal. Females are endowed with vapor, and this vapor is the source of fertility. The process in which generative essence is transformed into semen is called the path of forward move-ment; this path is the way of humankind and mortality. It is possi-ble, however, to direct generative essence and vapor back into the body and use them to nourish the body. The process of rout-ing generative energy back into the body is called the path of re-verse movement; it is this path that will lead us to the elixir of immortality.

The pre-celestial vapor is the true lead. This true lead of pre-celestial existence is needed to transform the post-celestial true mercury back into its pre-celestial state. Like two lovers, mother and son, or husband and wife, the two substances cannot bear to be separated from each other. This is the natural way of things. If you don't understand these principles, you'll never experience the thunder of yin and yang copulating in the grotto or penetrate the secrets of creation and transformation.

6

Primordial Generative Energy, Vapor, and Spirit

The primordial vapor is the true lead, and the primordial generative energy is the true mercury. But what is the primordial spirit? The primordial spirit is the master of original nature, generative energy, and vital energy. The primordial spirit is omniscient and unfathomable and is not confined to a location in the body. The foundation of all existence, it is called the spirit of life. When spirit is present, generative energy will be plentiful. When generative energy is plentiful, vapor will return to its proper place. When vapor is kept in its proper place, the elixir will be formed. Such are the workings of pre-celestial existence.

The primordial generative energy is not the generative energy spent during sexual intercourse but the true generative fluid hidden in the center of li. The primordial vapor is not equivalent to the breath we inhale and exhale but the true vital energy (vapor) hidden in the center of kan. The primordial spirit is not the thinking and conceptualizing mind but the spirit that is connected to the Limitless *(wuji)*. It is the numinous spark of truth that existed before the beginning of time.

Our bodies embody the Great Ultimate (taiji). Generative essence and vapor are the yin and yang that make up the Great Ultimate, and spirit is equivalent to the Limitless that is above and beyond the Great Ultimate. Together, these three are the generative, vital, and spirit energies in their primordial state. The poem "Jade Void" says: "The true generative energy is not the seminal fluid but the saliva from the mouth of the Jade Emperor." The Jade Emperor is none other than the ruler of the mind, and the saliva in his mouth is the numinous fluid. The true vapor is not the breath we inhale and exhale but the nectar of the Great Simplicity, and the Great Simplicity is none other than the vapor of primordial pre-celestial existence. The true spirit is not the mind that thinks about emptiness but the primordial lord of all things known as the Great Beginning.

The Great Beginning has no limits. Because it is limitless, it pervades the sky and earth and all things. Honored above all, it transcends the mundane and is the force that creates and transforms the universe.

7

The Spirit Is the Ruler

It is said that the spirit is the ruler of generative energy and vapor. Why? Because when the spirit is timid, generative energy will weaken and dissipate. When the spirit is desirous, vapor will leave and the body will tire easily. Spirit is hidden within generative energy. When its presence is strong, generative energy is said to have "spirit strength" *(jingshen)*. Spirit is also embedded within vapor. When its presence is commanding, vapor is said to have "vital spirit" *(shenqi)*. If spirit commands generative energy and vapor, the situation is analogous to a ruler being honored and served by his ministers. Therefore, those who cultivate the Tao must nurture the spirit.

Spirit is part of original nature. When original nature is still, spirit will naturally be stable. When the spirit is stable, generative energy will not dissipate. When generative energy does not dissipate, vapor will be plentiful. Why? It is because when original nature is not excited, the fire of the heart will not be fanned. When fire is not excited, water will not dry up. Consequently, generative energy will stay within the body. The essences of the five viscera and six bowels are watery in nature. When generative energy does not leak out, the essence of the kidneys will be strong. The kidneys store generative energy. When the kidneys are filled with generative energy, water will become a tidal force, rising up like clouds and mist to moisten the four great rivers above and below. If you can direct the spirit to aid the movement of water, then the processes of rising and falling, moving and stopping will be as easy as turning your hand. This phenomenon is what the alchemical texts refer to as "water and fire copulating and becoming harmonious." When post-celestial vapor meets water and fire, you will feel as if intoxicated. These processes all occur in post-celestial existence. I have yet to mention anything about pre-celestial existence.

When you have completed these post-celestial procedures, you will be ready to gather energy using techniques of sexual alchemy. Once you have gathered sufficient energy, the body will develop a new shell. The newborn shell will nourish the spirit, and in time the spirit will be able to merge with the oneness of the void. All these internal transformations occur naturally without active intervention from the spirit. This is why those who cultivate the Tao must refine the spirit, and refining the spirit means refining the jade fluid within. It is only by refining the jade fluid that you can become one with the beginning and end of the great Tao.

8

The Golden Elixir and the Jade Elixir

There are two elixirs: the golden elixir and the jade elixir. The golden elixir is used to refine the mind, and the jade elixir is used to refine the body. Why do we need to attain both elixirs? This is because to attain the Tao we must transform both spirit and body. What is meant by jade elixir? It is called the jade elixir because, like jade, it is warm, moist, virgin, and pure. What is meant by golden elixir? It is called the golden elixir because, like gold, it is strong and indestructible.

In cultivating the body, the goal is to chip away self-centeredness and greed so that we can realize the warm, moist, and virgin purity within. Jade symbolizes virtue, and when virtue is cultivated, the internal medicine will mature. When the internal medicine matures, the cauldron can be used to gather the medicine. After circulating the medicine for three hours, the wheel will begin to turn. When the wheel is set in motion, kan can be extracted and used to replenish li, and mercury can be collected and tamed. How is the golden elixir used to cultivate the mind in order to transform the body? When the golden elixir is cultivated, form takes on the qualities of pure yang, and the body will last forever. Like gold, it will be strong and indestructible. These transformations are what the internal alchemists refer to as "refining the golden and jade elixirs to cultivate body and mind in order to realize form and spirit."

The path of cultivating the jade elixir works with the form-less, while the path of cultivating the golden elixir works with form. The path of the formless is used to reach the path of form, but once the path of form is complete, we must return to the path of the formless again. These are the underlying principles of culti-vating mind and body. They are the surest way of attaining the sa-cred within.

9

Original Nature and Life

What is original nature? What is life? Original nature is the source of all things, and life (energy) is an integral part of the body. Without life, original nature cannot be nourished, and without original nature, life will lose its spirit. Original nature is the ruler of life, and life is the carrier of original nature. Many people today mistakenly classify spiritual practices into those that cultivate original nature and those that cultivate life, believing that these two paths are mutually exclusive. This is because they don't understand that spirit and life both originate from the Tao, that being and nonbeing are complements of each other, and that substance and nothingness cocreate each other.

Original nature is spirit, and life is generative and vital energy. Original nature is the Limitless (wuji), and life is the Great Ultimate (taiji). Each cannot exist without the other. Some say that Buddhists cultivate only original nature and Taoists cultivate only life. They are wrong, because they don't know that the Buddhist teachings of dissolving the self and eradicating desire are equivalent to the Taoist practice of holding on to the Mother and valuing the emptiness of the Great Beginning.

If you don't understand original nature, you won't be able to understand life. On the other hand, if you don't cultivate life, you won't be able to recover original nature. If you are able to prevent original nature from falling into oblivion, you will recover life. If you can hold on to the Mother and return to simplicity, you will nourish original nature. The cultivation of original nature is the key to entering the gate of life. This is what the wondrous method of focusing the spirit and merging with the true reality is all about.

After I understood the relationship of original nature and life, I asked my teacher how original nature is manifested in us and if it is tangible. My teacher told me that original nature is invisible and intangible. That which is visible and tangible is not the real original nature. If we try to see the intangible, it will only distance us from original nature. Why? This is because original nature can be intuited only by an empty mind; it cannot be grasped by intention or action. The ancient sages used the words "great simplicity" to refer to that which is nameless, and the Yellow Emperor searched for the Mysterious Pearl in that which is formless. Throughout history, sages have tried to describe the secret principles of how humans are created.

This is what they told us:

The true essence of the Limitless and the numerics two and five of the generative essence merge to give birth to all things. Original nature is the manifestation of the Limitless, and life is the product of the numerics two and five of the generative essence. When these two numerics interact, a human fetus is formed. Before birth, the Limitless is undifferentiated and without image, name, sound, shape, and sense of smell. When the numerics two and five copulate, the spark of the spirit emerges. When spirit first emerges, there is no thought or action and no duality of fullness and emptiness. This is original nature in its natural state. When feelings of desire arise, however, original nature will no longer remain in its primordial state. Zhang Boduan said, "After form emerges, original nature is manifested as vapor. If you are adept at the method of reversal, the original nature of heaven and earth can be preserved." Feelings and thoughts are tangible manifestations of vital energy. The primordial ways of heaven and earth are also manifestations of the energy of original nature. Laozi taught that we should return to simplicity, because it is through simplicity that we can return to the state of an infant and merge with the Limitless. This is the key to the path of reversal.

Those who cultivate the Tao should refine original nature. When original nature is still and vital energy is not taxed, the Limitless can be attained. My teacher once told me: "If original nature is not led astray, it will be still. When original nature is still, vital energy will return to its vaporous state. When vapor is returned to its original state, the elixir will emerge." The key to the return to the origin lies in introducing kan to li in the cauldron. When the post-celestial substance meets the pre-celestial, the wondrous method can be applied. This is what is meant by using original nature to unlock the gate of life.

10

Manifested Original Nature

There is true original nature and there is manifested original nature. True original nature is pre-celestial and clear, pure, round, and bright. Those who are intelligent do not have more of it, and those who are dull-witted do not have less of it. Manifested original nature is post-celestial and is born of vapor. As such, it can be clear or muddy, great or less. This is especially so when the numerics two and five merge to create humans and the ten thousand myriad things. In the process of creation, differences emerge. If all things come from the same source, why do differences exist? This is because as we move away from the primal beginning, desire increasingly takes control of the root of life. Feelings arise when we interact with the world, and, in time, vapor will be contaminated. Consequently, depending on their level of desire, people will exhibit differences in manifested original nature. The differences cannot be attributed to differences in original nature because original nature knows no differences.

In its manifested form, original nature is often used to serve selfish interests. This is not the kind of original nature we should cultivate. Only the spirit of true original nature should be cultivated. If the manifested original nature rules, we will have the situation of the servant controlling the master.

Original nature is like water. When degraded into manifested vital energy, it is analogous to water draining into mud. We cannot turn the muddy puddle into a clear pool overnight. However, in time, mud and water will separate. The mud will sink to the bottom and the clear water stay at the surface. Knowing how to separate the clear from the muddy is the key to the process of reversal and recovering life.

II

The Chamber of the Spirit

Are original nature and primordial spirit different? No. Because original nature is numinous, omniscient, fathomless, and omnipotent, we call it spirit. Because we need to contrast it with the thinking and conceptualizing mind of post-celestial existence, we refer to it as primordial.

Does the spirit have a home? When I asked my teacher Ziqing, he told me that the spirit dwells in three valleys in our body. We describe the spirit's dwelling places as valleys because they are empty like a hollow in the land. Thus, the spirit that dwells in the valley is called the valley spirit. When the spirit is in its home, it will give birth to other spirit forms; when the spirit leaves its home permanently, we will die. When the spirit is restless and unable to stay peacefully in its home, it will be led astray by attachments during the day and run amok in dreams at night. The medical text *Spiritual Pivot (Lingshu)* tells us: "The primordial spirit lives in the Celestial Valley within the body of the realized being." The Celestial Valley is the upper valley, and it is synonymous with the Mudball *(niwan)* cavity. The middle valley is synonymous with the Crimson Palace *(jianggong)* cavity. The lower valley is the Spirit Valley, and it is synonymous with the Primal Gate *(guanyuan)* cavity. The spirit resides in all three valleys. Therefore, the valleys are often referred to as the three elixir fields. The Mudball cavity is the original home of the spirit; the Crimson Palace cavity is where the spirit receives reports from its subordinates and gives audiences; and the Spirit Valley is the hermitage where the spirit cultivates itself in secret.

When the primordial spirit is in the Crimson Palace cavity, the ears and eyes will be alert. The five viscera and the senses will carry out orders, and the limbs and joints will follow without hesitation. When the primordial spirit is in the Spirit Valley, the senses will be drawn inward, spirit and vital energy will be gathered, and the One will be embraced by the soul within. A sage once said, "When the heart is hidden in deep water, the root of the spirit will be exquisite beyond measure." By deep water, we mean that which is fathomless and unpredictable. This deep and fathomless place is the Spirit Valley, the primordial spirit's secret hiding place.

12

The Waterwheel

To hide the spirit is to return to the root. Returning to the root means holding on to stillness, and holding on to stillness means recovering life. When you begin to feel spirit and vapor merging and embracing each other, it is a sign that stillness has reached its height and movement is about to begin. When movement occurs, the spirit will be carried by vapor, and together vapor and spirit will surge up to the Mudball cavity. At this time, the path of the waterwheel will open.

The path of the waterwheel is the circuit formed by the ren and du meridians. When vapor ascends, it will be moistened and steamed in the area between the kidneys. Like waves rolling onto a sandy shore, it will soak and flood the five viscera before gushing through the channels to spread throughout the body. When you feel the beginnings of movement, you must direct the spirit immediately into the Tailbone *(weilu)* cavity. From the Tailbone cavity, let the spirit rise to the cavity between the shoulder blades, then through the Wind House *(fengfu)* cavity, and finally into the Mudball cavity. When spirit and vapor copulate in the Mudball cavity, vapor will flow through the body without obstruction. A little later, you will feel a substance tasting like fresh, sweet nectar descending. Falling from the Pagoda down to the Crimson Palace cavity and into the Purple Pavilion *(ziting)* cavity, it will return to where it originated and come to rest. In time, this circulatory movement will become effortless, and the three elixir fields (dantiens) will be filled with vapor. When vapor is plentiful, it will swirl around and push through the joints to spread throughout the body. Generative energy will now be plentiful, and the valley spirit will never die. When you have reached this level of cultivation, the effects of the internal transformations will be clear. If you haven't reached this state of development, however, any discussion of the waterwheel is just empty talk.

13

Purifying the Spirit

After I learned about the hiding place of the spirit, I realized that spirit and life energy are intertwined. When I asked about the meaning of hiding the spirit, I was told that hiding the spirit meant focusing the spirit. To focus the spirit, we must purify the spirit, and to purify the spirit we must get rid of desire. *Cultivating Stillness (Qingjingjing)* states: "Get rid of desire and the mind will be still naturally. Purify the mind and the spirit will be clear naturally." The *Triplex Unity* states: "The sage cleans the mind and retreats to hide it in secret."

Cleaning the mind means purifying the mind. Zhou Dunyi said, "When there are no desires, there will be stillness." Absence of desire means getting rid of desires until they no longer exist. The spirit in us tends toward clarity but is disturbed by the mind. The mind tends toward stillness but is led astray by desires.

There are two aspects of mind. First, there is the mind that disturbs the spirit: This is the wayward mind. Second, there is the mind that tends toward stillness: This is the true mind. When the wayward mind dominates, it will disturb the spirit. When the spirit is disturbed, it will become attached to the ten thousand things. When the mind clings to the ten thousand things, all kinds of desires will arise. When desires arise, anxiety will also arise. Anxiety and thoughts can weaken both body and mind. When anxiety is present, how can the mind be still? This is why we need to get rid of desire if we want to purify the spirit. When desire is absent, mind will not be present when you gaze into mind.

When you look at forms externally, know that the forms have no form. When you look at things in the world, know that things have no substance. If you let go of the senses, both mind and self will be empty. There will be nothing in emptiness and nothing in nothingness. When nothingness is empty, absolute stillness will never leave you. When stillness is not cognized as stillness, all methods and principles will become empty. The roots will be pure, the six sensual phenomena will not emerge, and the mind will always be still. When the mind is still, the spirit will be clear and calm like the smooth surface of a lake.

Master Xuijing said, "If you want to hold the spirit within the body, you must not leave even a speck of dust on the spirit altar." If there are objects in the mind, the spirit will not be clear. When spirit is disturbed, the true generative energy will escape, and the tendons and bones will be damaged. The teachings of dissolving desire and purifying the spirit as given by the sages are not much different from what I have just enumerated.

14

Nourishing the Spirit

How can the spirit be enhanced after it has been purified? We can enhance the spirit by nourishing it. Nourishing the spirit means gathering the spirit's light and drawing it inward. The spirit has substance. The purer it is, the clearer it will be; the clearer it is, the brighter it will be. The sage Zhuangzi said, "When the universe is in harmony, it will glow like the bright sky." Wisdom is born from stillness. When the numinous light emerges, you must hide it by drawing it within. If you expose it by displaying or using it recklessly, original nature will be injured. Again Zhuangzi said, "The ancient followers of the Tao cultivated wisdom in quietude." Wisdom is true intelligence, and it emerges when mundane intelligence dissolves. This is what is meant by using quietude to cultivate true intelligence. The *Treatise on the Pivotal Method of Sitting and Forgetting (Zuowangshuyilun)* states: "Attain wisdom but do not display it. Be intelligent but appear dim-witted. Use your abilities to stabilize wisdom." The *Tao Te Ching* states: "Genuine and sincere, the sage is simple and content; undifferentiated, he merges with the muddy world," and "Everyone wants to outshine everybody else; I alone want to be dull and common. Everyone wants to see everything there is to see; I alone prefer to be uninterested." This is what nourishing the spirit is all about.

15

Focusing the Spirit

———

Why do we need to focus the spirit after it has been nourished? It is because when we focus the spirit, that which is functionless is used to serve function. Thus, focusing the spirit is integral to the art of recovering life. When the *Triplex Unity* instructs us to "nurture the processes of opening and closing to realize the true body," it is referring to cultivating stillness in the palace of li. The practice is similar to Chan sitting and is the foundation for attaining the mysterious subtleties in the house of water. Once the spirit is purified, you must focus it quickly. The author of the treatise *Jade Emptiness (Zuixui)* said, "When my teacher gave me the oral teachings, he told me that the key lies in focusing the spirit and drawing it into the cavity of the vapor." The cavity of the vapor is where opening and closing occurs. This was explained in the chapter entitled "The Chamber of the Spirit."

Many students know about purifying the spirit but don't know where to direct the spirit so that it can be focused. If you don't know where to lead the spirit, the spirit will wander aimlessly and never be able to return home. As a result, it cannot go back to the root to meet the source that renews life. If you don't know where to focus the spirit, you will not be able to initiate the wondrous and subtle process of transformation. This is why I have decided to share what I have learned from my teachers, so that you can learn to focus the spirit and lead it to the mysterious subtleties.

The ancient sages have laid down the following principles on focusing the spirit. First, focusing the spirit does not simply mean keeping it still. Rather, it means directing the spirit into the cavity of the vapor, holding it there, and not letting spirit and vapor separate. Laozi said, "In nurturing the spirit and holding on to the One, can you prevent them from separating?" The cavity of the vapor is where we first receive the vapor of the Tao when we were conceived in our mother's womb. It is where the generative energy of our father and the vapor of our mother merged. Thus, the taiji is embodied within all of us. The cavity of the vapor has many names. It has been called the Sea of Vapor *(qihai)*, the Gate of the Origin *(guanyuan)*, the Numinous Valley *(ninggu)*, the Lower Elixir Field *(xiatien)*, the Celestial Root *(tiengun)*, the Stem of Life *(mingdi)*, the Cavity of Returning to the Root *(guigunjiao)*, and the Gate to Recovering Life *(fomingguan)*. These names all refer to the location where the breath of the fetus is connected to the mother. When the infant leaves the womb and the umbilical cord is cut, the child will develop its furnace and cauldron and erect its own sky (qian) and earth (kun).

Second, focusing the spirit means anchoring the life energy by letting each inhalation and exhalation return to its origin. If the breath is not connected to its origin during inhalation and exhalation, the breath of life will be extinguished, and we will die. In exhalation, the breath needs to open to allow the essence of yang to circulate smoothly. In inhalation, the breath must close to conserve the essence of yin. One exhalation and one inhalation make up one cycle of breath. Even those in the healing professions know that regulation of breath is good for health. Zhuangzi said, "The common person breathes through the throat; thus, his breath is shallow. In contrast, the realized being does not breathe through the throat; thus, his breath is heavy." By heavy, we mean that the breath sinks deep into the cavity of the vapor. The ordinary person's breath is never heavy because the spirit is not present in the breath. As a result, when the breath enters and exits, it only reaches the throat. On the other hand, the breath of the realized being is merged with the spirit so that both breath and spirit can penetrate deep into the cavity of the vapor. When spirit resides in the vapor, the breath will never be broken. It is for this reason that the breath of the realized being is soft and secure; it is always embracing the One and never leaving it. When the spirit abides in absolute stillness, the spirit can see the path of the return.

Third, focusing the spirit means merging breath and spirit. This is *not* equivalent to using the spirit to chase or drive the movement of breath. The role of the spirit is to help the breath to move without forcing it to go one way or the other. When spirit is merged with breath, spirit will be focused. When spirit is focused, vapor will also be focused. When spirit is merged with breath, spirit will be harmonious. When spirit is harmonious, vapor will also be harmonious. This is the principle of the symbiotic relationship of spirit and breath.

Thus, focusing the spirit begins with regulating the breath, and regulating the breath means merging it with the spirit.

The True Breath

There are two kinds of breath: mundane breath and true breath. Mundane breath is the breath that goes through the mouth and nostrils. True breath is the fetal breath that rises and falls within the cavity of the Origin. Master Huiweng described the true breath as "sealed inside emptiness like a fish in spring waters." When mundane breath stops, true breath will move naturally. The mundane breath stops not because we force it to do so but because absolute stillness and emptiness are present. As the presence of mind grows less and less, the breath will become increasingly soft. Many people talk about regulating the breath but don't know where the breath should be directed to. It is dangerous to use the mind to push the breath. The ordinary mind is temperamental and wild and must be tamed before it can follow the breath naturally. The mind cannot be forced to merge with the breath. Otherwise, intention will be too strong. When intention is overly strong, the vapor will not be still. When vapor is not still, how can the vapor embrace the spirit?

Regulating the breath means letting the mind follow the breath naturally. It does not mean forcing the mind to chase after the breath. Regulating the breath begins with taming the mind, and taming the mind means getting rid of desire and returning to stillness. Returning to stillness means maintaining emptiness in walking, sitting, sleeping, and all everyday activities. With time and practice, entering and maintaining stillness will become natural.

The hard ice will turn soft, and mind and breath will be harmonious. When mind and breath are in harmony, they will embrace each other. When they embrace but do not cling to each other, the mundane breath will stop and the true breath will move. When the true breath moves, the bellows will be fanned and generative energy will be transmuted into vital energy. Rising like steam, the vapor of vital energy will fill the Three Palaces. When this occurs, the true bellows, true cauldron, true furnace, and true fire will emerge.

17

The Firing Schedule

Many think that the true breath is fire. It is true that we need to attend to the medicinal furnace and watch the fire patiently. However, we also need to still the spirit and let it follow the breath naturally. If you attend the stove vigilantly, the waterwheel, the crane's womb, and the tortoise's breath will swirl constantly. The ancient sages have described this process in different ways, but they all agreed that the breath is not identical to the true fire. The true fire is the sacred fire; the true breath is but the bellows that stoke the fire. When spirit and vapor are held together, the spirit will abide in nonaction, and the mechanism that drives the vapor will have no alternative but to move. Each opening and closing is synchronous with the upward and downward movement in the ren and du meridians. What is felt as moving is none other than the spirit. When the undifferentiated primal vapor flows without hindrance, the primordial spirit will feel it. If the correct amount of fire is applied, spirit and vapor will copulate and embrace each other. If the fire is stoked properly, the pill will materialize and the medicine will be complete.

The reason for equating the bellows with the true breath is obvious. Blacksmiths who temper and refine steel know that they must pump the bellows to stoke the fire. When the fire is ready, it can be used to heat and temper the steel. If you fan the fire by blowing with the mouth, the fire will be weak and erratic. Consequently, the metal cannot be tempered. Wind generated by blowing with the mouth is unreliable; it is like the shallow breath of the ordinary person. Wind fanned by the bellows is continuous; it is like the heavy sinking breath of the realized being. When spirit follows the breath and is merged with it, the bellows will be engaged and the fire will be fanned properly. When vapor is introduced to the spirit, it will be transformed naturally. I hope this analogy will help you understand the teachings.

When I asked my teacher about the principles of flow and ebb and what it means to collect in the morning and secure in the evening, he told me that it was only after he had received instructions from his teacher that he fully understood the meaning of the Celestial Circuit and the cyclical properties of the trigrams. Before he met his teacher, he had only partial information and understanding. As a result, he wasted much time in his early life trying to figure out what was going on. After he understood the teachings, he realized that there is no need to read the numerous texts that describe the six hundred or more meanings of applying fire.

The true fire has no schedule of application, and the great medicine has no weight or measure. This is the absolute truth. There is an outer and an inner process of refining the medicine, and there are simple and complex schedules of firing. Internal refining is continuous and elusive: It is there and yet not there. External refining, however, is more structured and is synchronized with the celestial and terrestrial cycles. In external refining, the firing schedule is mapped to the cycle of celestial movement. In the production of the elixir, the days *gen* and *jia* of the lunar month mark the time when the medicinal ingredients are mature, and the hours *zi* (11 P.M.–1 A.M.) and *wu* (11 A.M.–1 P.M.) refer to the daily cycle of the breath rising and falling respectively. As for the meaning of "collecting in the morning and securing in the evening," this refers to none other than the discipline of entering and exiting. Once you have understood these things, you will no longer need to refer back to the texts and their images.

Understanding Reality states: "The internal medicine must be circulated like the external medicine. Both the internal and external universes must be open." This means that the head of the pill must be harmonious with its partner, and both must be bathed and steamed together. Internally, the natural true fire must burn inside a furnace that is always red-hot. Externally, the ingredients must be added and subtracted carefully before the fire in the furnace is stoked. Work hard on acquiring the true seed, and know that the key to attaining the true seed lies in the correct application of fire in the human domain.

18

Medicine and Fire

Are medicine and fire the same entity?

Medicine and fire can be considered separate entities or merged as one. When separate, they are different; when merged, they are one and the same.

When medicine and fire are separate entities, medicine is the pre-celestial vapor and fire is the pre-celestial spirit. When merged, medicine is the fire, and fire is the medicine. If you know them only in their combined form and not as separate entities, you will not understand what it means to gather and collect. If you know them only as separate forms and not as a combined entity, you will not be able to understand the method of steaming and nourishing. Why? During the process of collecting, the medicine is outside and the fire is inside, and the fire is used to temper the medicine. In this condition, medicine and fire are separate. During the processes of steaming and nourishing, medicine from the outside is brought inside and fire is applied to it. In this condition, medicine and fire are merged. However, in both conditions, fire directs the course of events. If the fire is too hot, the elixir will be scorched; if the heat is insufficient, the elixir will dissipate. When fire is discussed in the absence of medicine, we are talking about the ten lunar months of incubation. When medicine is discussed in the absence of fire, we are talking about the hourly schedule of applying heat.

The immortal teacher Ziqing said that using fire to refine the medicine and transmuting it into the elixir is equivalent to using the spirit to lead vapor to return to the Tao.

19

Extracting and Replenishing

When I asked my teacher to explain the principle of extracting lead to replenish mercury, he told me that after Master Liyang had attained the medicine and directed it into the cauldron, he practiced extracting and replenishing to nourish the natural true fire so that it will never extinguish.

The process of extracting and replenishing must occur naturally. No force should be applied. This is because the Tao follows the way of nonaction, and spirit and vapor are naturally still. Herein lies the wondrous mystery of creation. I will use the analogy of cooking rice to explain the principles of extracting and replenishing. Introducing lead to mercury is like putting rice grains in water. The amount of water must not be excessive, and the amount of rice cannot be too little. When the correct amount of heat is applied, water will boil, and the grains will absorb water to become cooked rice. The extraction of lead is similar to water being absorbed by the rice. The process of replenishing mercury is similar to rice grains expanding when they absorb water. Therefore, strictly speaking, nothing is subtracted during extracting and nothing is added during replenishing. Spirit entering vapor is equivalent to the vapor of the sky descending to earth. When the essence of sky vapor enters the earth, it becomes part of the soil. Vapor embracing the spirit is equivalent to the vapor of earth receiving the vapor of the sky. When mist rises from the ground, it becomes part of the air in the atmosphere.

When extracting and replenishing are applied continuously, the fetus will grow. When the fetus matures, other bodily forms will appear beyond the corporeal body. These wondrous subtleties occur naturally without the interference of conscious knowledge or intention. Attend too much to the process of extracting and replenishing, and you will activate intention and thought. When thought and intention take hold, things are no longer natural. The meaning of being natural is difficult to grasp. The teachers said, "Move with what is natural; do not think about what is natural." This is the key to being natural.

20

Concluding Remarks

Why haven't I mentioned terms such as red lead, black mercury, green dragon, white tiger, white snow, yellow sprouts, the lord of wood, the mother of metal, the infant, and the yellow woman?

I urge you, reader, to listen patiently to what I have to say next. When I was a Confucian student, I tried to study the words and phrases of the alchemical texts as a scholar before I had any spiritual foundation and experience. All my efforts at study came to nothing. Then, I had the fortune of meeting a teacher of a true lineage. After receiving the teachings, I realized that I needed practice and experience before I could understand the meaning of the alchemical terms mentioned above. Now that I have learned their meanings, I realize that the Tao is not difficult to understand. In fact, we can explain it in a single sentence: The Tao is composed of one yin and one yang, where yin is the generative essence, yang is the vapor, and spirit is their ruler. This is why spirit, vapor, and generative essence are regarded as the three great medicines. The names dragon, tiger, lead, and mercury were used by the immortals and sages to hide the true meanings from unethical practitioners. As a result, many names have been given to the same cavity or the same substance. Because different people focus on different aspects of the teachings, there are now many lineages and schools. Unfortunately, this diversity has often led students to focus on words alone. Trying to understand the alchemical terms intellectually, they end up missing the true meaning. If you want to penetrate the meanings of the alchemical terms easily and naturally, you must build a strong foundation and practice diligently, because the root of all meanings can be attained only through practice.

Why does this text talk about the external medicine in detail but not describe how energy is gathered from a sexual partner? The techniques of sexual alchemy are secret teachings. Given to a select few by the celestial deities, they can only be transmitted directly from teacher to student. It is not because I don't want to describe them; it's because I can't disobey my teachers' orders. Throughout this text I was careful not to reveal the highest secrets. It may appear that I have broken my oath of secrecy, but if you look carefully, none of the highest secret teachings has been revealed.

The *Triplex Unity* states: "There are many wondrous subtleties, but to 'see' them you must study them tens of thousands of times." Thus, students of the Tao must study the materials again and again before they can intuit the mysterious wonders. Don't be discouraged or frustrated if you feel you haven't understood anything after years of study and practice. The internal transformations described in this text are not easy to attain. However, if and when you finally grasp the subtle meanings and penetrate the essence of the teachings, you will experience a joy beyond understanding.

Discussion on the Cavity of the Tao

(DAOJIAOTAN)

Translator's note: Li Xiyue is also known as Duanyang, Duanyangzi, and Li Hanxui. *Daojiaotan* is a compilation of talks given by Li Xiyue. This explains the sections of questions and answers and long quotations of Duanyang's teachings.

I

Some Advice for Friends

When you meditate, it is important that you enter and maintain stillness naturally. Find a small hut in a quiet place. Sleep on a bed of bamboo. Rise in the wee hours of the morning, cross your legs, and sit in stillness. When the session is over, uncross your legs slowly before standing up. All these actions should be natural. This advice is given to anyone who is willing to listen.

The air is clear at night. This makes it the best time to regulate the breath and still the spirit. When you regulate the breath, you should be patient and not have preconceptions of what it means to be empty and still. When the breath begins to slow and then stop, you should not be attached to it. Don't try to direct it or remind yourself to forget it. The breath should be there and yet not there. Even in absolute stillness, you should be alert and be aware of everything. When the mind is bright and clear, the following processes will occur naturally: The water will be clear, the fire will be ignited, the spirit will be focused, the vapor will be gathered, and the waterwheel will move. Extracting and replenishing will occur, and the cycles of flow and ebb will be timely. However, before these wondrous things can happen, the restless mind must be tamed. When mind is still, ignorance will disappear, and the wayward mind will return to its home.

It is easy to be lethargic or be fearful of the light within. If you feel sleepy while meditating, you should take control of yourself immediately. Don't think that you can stay awake by shaking your body or rubbing your eyes. I won't give you further instructions until you have cultivated discipline. You must be able to stop your internal chatter the moment you close your eyes. I will wait until your mind is clear before I instruct you further.

Being lethargic in the clear night is a sign of lack of discipline. Being restless in the stillness of the night is a sign of lack of focus in your practice. If you are lazy and distracted, you will dishonor the kindness and good intentions of your teacher. My ways can lead you to the subtlest of mysteries. Those who make these mistakes should correct them immediately.

2

Opening the Gates

Some students asked the sage Duanyang:

"We humbly ask you to tell us about the mysterious sub-tleties. Why do we need to purify the true substance within, re-cover simplicity, and open the One cavity when we first start to cultivate the Tao? We have heard the teachers Sun and Tao say that the gates and the One cavity must be open before the foundation can be built. The sage Qianxui, however, considered such matters secret and refused to talk about them. Today, many people main-tain that just as good horses are endowed with good bones, realiz-ing the great Tao is dependent largely on human effort. Therefore, we beg you to tell us how to open the gates and the One cavity."

Duanyangzi replied:

"The sage Qianxui was not trying to hide information. What he meant was that those who have lost the pre-celestial clarity and stillness will have to use the lesser techniques to cultivate life en-ergy. Nonaction is the highest virtue. If you hadn't broken your pre-celestial body, you would have been able to practice the method of single cultivation and realize the immortal fetus in no time. This path of returning to the Tao is easy because there's no need to open gates that have been closed. The method of single cultivation is the most direct path to the Tao. Laozi said that when the great Tao no longer rules, we'll have to rely on virtues like honor and integrity to maintain harmony. If you look at the meth-ods of cultivation taught today, you'll find that they are suitable only for those who have not broken their pre-celestial body. My method of opening the gates and the cavity, however, is for those who have lost their virginity. This method allows practitioners to progress quickly on the road of the return to the origin. The key to this approach lies in using a partner to repair your body and recover the true substance within.

"If you begin cultivation after middle age, you'll need to learn how to focus the spirit, regulate the breath, and direct the vapor of yin into the cauldron. Be alert while directing the vapor into your body. Most important, do not use effort. When the post-celestial vapor emerges, regulate and steam it, and the true wheel will begin to move. When you feel movement, channel the vapor along its course gently. Do not use force. In time, the gates will open, and the One cavity will expand naturally. When the true vapor rises to the Mudball (niwan) cavity, the path of the water-wheel will be open. Everything must occur naturally. In the transition between movement and stillness, fan the fire gently, route the vapor through the Tailbone (weilu) cavity, and let it flow backward (and thus upward) into the Celestial Valley (tiengu) cavity. In this way, generative energy will be transmuted into vapor. When the vapor waxes strong, it will fill the three palaces. Later, when you collect the wondrous medicine from the outside, you'll be able to capture the true vapor within your own body. Swirling inside, the vapor will not dissipate or become disorderly. Once you have attained the true vapor, you should protect it like two lovers caring for each other, like a dragon nourishing its pearl, or like a hen incubating her eggs. In time, the vapor will descend to the Yellow Pavilion to coagulate into a bright red ball known as the internal pill. When you have attained the pill, the beginning stage of your cultivation will be complete. You can now enjoy longevity and begin to work on preserving your bodily form."

My friends were delighted when they heard Duanyanzi's response. They bowed and said, "Most honorable teacher, your teachings have removed a lot of obstacles. Your humble students now ask for your permission to leave and practice what you have taught."

3

The Meaning of Post-celestial

In the past, post-celestial methods have been divided into those involved with building the foundation and those involved with refining the body. However, Master Tao said that if the gates are not open, then talking about building the foundation and refining the body is like trying to relieve an itch by scratching with a piece of soft leather. You'll spend a lot of effort but gain nothing. To help practitioners understand what is involved in cultivating the Tao, the Master separated the stages of cultivation into four steps—opening the gates, building the foundation, obtaining the medicine, and refining the body—and called them post-celestial techniques. Because it is easy to misunderstand these techniques, I will now explain them to you.

In the past, practitioners have delineated two stages of cultivation. For clarification, I have followed Master Tao's scheme of breaking the two stages into four steps. The first step, opening the gates, is the prerequisite for building the foundation (the second step). The third step is obtaining the medicine, which is the prerequisite for strengthening the foundation. The fourth step is refining the body, and it is the key to completing the foundation. These four steps are subsumed under two stages, and the two stages are subsumed under the one (post-celestial) approach.

The ancient sages have said repeatedly that they do not want to reveal the details of the techniques trivially and that only those who are virtuous can attain the Tao. Although post-celestial techniques of building the foundation and refining the body do not constitute the highest methods of cultivation, they have been revered and discussed by others before Master Tao. The *Triplex Unity* states: "Action belongs to the domain of lower virtue and can be used continuously. Because that which is used cannot be exhausted, you can apply it frequently." How you interpret the meaning of these words will depend on your intuition and depth of understanding.

Immortal Luan said, "If you want to cultivate the Tao, you must first use the cauldron to open the gate. The cauldron is none other than the spirit father and spirit mother." Why is the cauldron referred to as the spirit parents? It is because they are the father and mother that give birth to the immortal and the Buddha in us. The spirit parents should not be confused with the birth father and mother. The spirit father and spirit mother make up the post-celestial cauldron. In copulation, they follow the path of reversal. In contrast, when our earthly father and mother copulate, they follow the forward path to create a life form. In the path of reversal, female and male are in embrace from the beginning to the end. After the cauldron is erected, spirit and vapor can copulate. When spirit and vapor copulate, both spirit and vital energy will accumulate. When these two substances are plentiful, their thrusting power will be great. When the thrusting power is great, they can open the gates and enlarge the One cavity. When the gates and the One cavity are open, the movement of reversal can begin and the waterwheel can turn.

Turning the waterwheel, however, is not part of the process of opening the gates. The key to opening the gates lies in using the post-celestial true vapor correctly, while the key to working the waterwheel lies in moving the post-celestial golden water. When the waterwheel turns naturally, there is no difference between moving the waterwheel and strengthening the foundation. The sage Qianxui said, "Circulate and soak simultaneously. In time, practice will become perfect, and vapor will fill the three dantiens. The upper and lower will copulate and harmonize; vapor will thrust through the joints and penetrate the bones; and generative energy will fill the valley spirit." I have often mentioned that the post-celestial method is a reliable way to nourish the body. If you understand my humble teachings and recognize that this method embodies the four steps mentioned above, you will attain health and longevity.

What is meant by nourishing the body? The *Triplex Unity* states: "Internally, cultivate the body with stillness and emptiness." This is an important aspect of the post-celestial method. Body is an integral part of original nature or primordial spirit. By internal, we mean the universe within. When there is emptiness within, there will be stillness and inner peace. When there is inner peace, true wisdom will arise. If you can enter and maintain stillness, you can resonate with the universe. If you want to still the spirit, you must regulate the breath. One inhalation and one exhalation constitute one breath. To regulate the breath means that inhalation and exhalation must be natural and moving without intervention. The *Zhuangzi* says, "The breath of the realized being is heavy." By heavy, we mean that the breath sinks low and is barely felt. When the breath sinks low, vapor will penetrate the Bubbling Spring *(yongquan)* cavity and will flow in and out continuously. My teacher said, "Use the internal breath to move the external breath, and use the external breath to move the internal breath. Using breath to move breath is the key to the wondrous subtleties." When regulating the breath, internal and external inhalation should be coupled together. It is when the internal and external breaths are synchronized that they can give birth to each other. When the cycle of opening and closing is timely and regular, wondrous and subtle things will happen naturally.

In the past, many teachers have said that students must understand the function of the bellows and the structure of the Mysterious Gate *(xuanmen)* before they can build the foundation. However, let me tell you this: If you understand the meaning of internal breathing, you will know how to use the bellows naturally. The internal alchemists all say that during exhalation the breath should not exit the nostrils, and during inhalation the breath must be drawn into the navel. True internal breathing is initiated in the navel. After you have activated internal breathing and after the breath has slowed down and become regular, you should focus the spirit. To focus the spirit means to enter stillness and turn the gaze within. Focusing the spirit and regulating breath cannot be accomplished in a short time. Therefore, you must be patient. When the breath is regulated, the spirit will return. When the spirit returns, the gaze will turn inward naturally. When the gaze is turned inward, vapor will be born. When vapor emerges, you should capture and secure it within. When the vapor is secure, it will accumulate. Once sufficient vapor is accumulated, the internal golden cauldron will be filled with light. The primordial yellow will swirl and tumble within, and the true vapor will penetrate the heart and enter the Tailbone cavity. As vapor rushes through the three gates, the path connecting the cowherd and weaving maiden will be open. The silver stream will be connected, and the secret techniques of cultivation will be open to you.

Regulating the breath, focusing the spirit, gathering the vapor, thrusting open the gates, building the foundation, and refining the self are all part of the process of nourishing the body. The sage Shangyang said, "Nourishing the body means treasuring generative energy and harvesting the vapor. Refining the self means forgetting desire and severing attachments to the external world." Refining the self is the internal support for nourishing the body. The processes of nourishing the body and refining the self are interrelated. If you refine the self but do not cultivate the body, the foundation of the elixir will not be completed. If you cultivate the body but do not refine the self, the essence of mercury cannot be secured. If you want to cultivate the body, you must harvest and use another person's lead. This lead is the pre-celestial essence hidden within post-celestial existence. The post-celestial golden water has vitality but lacks the essence of pre-celestial existence. When the true lead first emerges, it must be steamed in the area between the kidneys. When you feel the lead stirring, you must start the waterwheel, temper and refine it, and send it to the Tailbone cavity. From the Tailbone cavity, direct the refined lead up to the Celestial Valley cavity, where it will be transformed into sweet nectar. Finally, let the sweet nectar sink into the Yellow Pavilion *(huangting)*. After the true lead has moistened the three palaces, it will be used to transform mercury. When vapor is transmuted into fluid, the yin fire will ebb and the pearl drops will not dissipate. When the fluid is transmuted back into vapor, it is time to stoke the yang fire and turn the water-wheel again. When the waterwheel is turning, do not forget to continue to refine original nature by taming the mind and sweeping away the dust of the world. It is said that by stilling body and mind, the great sage can harmonize his internal light with the mundane and therefore live comfortably in the city or in the mountains and forests. When the mercury within is secure and stable, you should take eight ounces of the pre-celestial essence to complement the half pound of the post-celestial substance. When you have reached this stage of cultivation, you are ready to ask about the method of circulating the internal pill.

4

Building the Foundation and Refining the Self

Building the foundation and refining the self can be considered two parts of one process. The first part involves building the lesser and greater foundations; the second part involves refining the self externally and internally.

What is involved in building the lesser foundation? Typically, building the lesser foundation is concerned with the following practices: gathering the primordial yang energy and directing it into the internal cauldron, gently engaging fetal breathing, producing the post-celestial medicine, and activating the process of refining the jade. These practices are described by Masters Tao and Sun as "obtaining the medicine after completing the foundation" and "refining the self after collecting the internal medicine."

What is involved in building the greater foundation? Typically, building the greater foundation is concerned with the following practices: nourishing the numinous pearl to give birth to the external lead, churning the golden water, activating the subtle movement of the Microcosmic Orbit, and recovering original nature. These practices are equivalent to what I have described in the previous chapter as opening the gate to begin building the foundation, obtaining the medicine to continue building the foundation, and refining the self to finish building the foundation.

Internal refining of the self is concerned with the work of the waterwheel. According to the *Triplex Unity,* the production of the jade elixir is necessary for refining the body internally, which is different from refining the self externally. In refining the self externally, the goal is to see all things as empty and not allow even a speck of dust to accumulate. The sages describe it as letting go of attachments in the midst of the world. In refining the self internally, the goal is to build the greater foundation, which is integral to nourishing the body. This is why I have considered building the foundation and refining the self as one process divided into two parts. I hope students of the Tao understand this clearly.

5

Nourishing the Body and Refining the Self (Part 1)

I mentioned earlier that nourishing the body is part of the process of refining the self internally. However, refining the self involves practices other than nourishing the body. I will discuss each in turn.

The process of external refining of the self involves tempering the mind in the midst of the world. In this way, it is different from both internal refining of the self and nourishing the body. External refining is concerned with refining the mind until it is naturally still. When the mind is still, the body will also be still. When the body is still, sexual desire cannot shake it, and wealth and power will not be able to bind it. As a result, the true mercury will be retained and the foundation of the pill will be strengthened.

There are similarities between refining the self internally and nourishing the body. Some texts equate refining the self internally with the process of steaming the mercury and transforming it into red cinnabar. However, Master Tao said, "Refining the self is not just getting something out of nothing." And the sage Shangyang said, "It is easy to cultivate the pill but difficult to refine the self."

By self, we mean the true mercuric fire. First, we must temper the true fire and conquer the true dragon, so that both fire and dragon will follow our command willingly and not wander away. Next, we need to tame the white tiger and obtain its precious true metal. These two processes are equivalent to what I have described as refining the self internally and nourishing the body.

When you use the paired method (which is working with a consort), the process of refining the self internally is concerned with using your partner's lead to refine your mercury and letting them mutually control and create each other. In the process of nourishing the body, the partner's lead is used to nourish your mercury so that lead and mercury can strengthen each other. These are the differences between refining the self internally and nourishing the body.

6

Nourishing the Body and Refining the Self (Part 2)

The practices concerned with nourishing the body and refining the self are closely related. To nourish the body is to conserve generative energy and strengthen vapor, or vital energy. Both generative energy and vapor are necessary for building the foundation. To refine the self is to dissolve desire and recover original nature. Nourishing the body is a prerequisite for refining the self. When generative energy and vapor are used to nourish the body, the foundation will be firm. Thus, if you want to build a solid foundation, you must nourish the body. In refining the self, we temper and tame the mind so that it is alert and bright. Original nature is manifested in mind. Therefore, to recover original nature, we must refine the self. Nourishing the body requires strengthening the generative and vital energies. Generative energy must be held inside when vital energy is absorbed from the outside. While it is the body that is nourished, it is the mind that is responsible for securing what is gathered.

Nourishing the body requires stillness and inner peace. I have divided the practice of nourishing the body into two aspects: single nourishing and dual nourishing. Dual nourishing works with generative and vital energies, while single nourishing works with inner peace and stillness. The process of refining the self needs to occur in the world of feelings, but we must not be attached to feelings and emotions. Although the external environment is perceived as empty, nonattachment must originate from the inside.

The mind must delight in emptiness and be free from worry, anxiety, and frustration.

The process of refining the self is concerned with knowing the functions of movement and stillness. I have divided the practice of refining the self into two aspects: internal refinement and external refinement. External refinement is concerned with harmonizing the light while merging with the mundane. Internal refinement is concerned with steaming mercury and transforming it into red cinnabar. The mnemonics say: "If you want to cultivate the true path, you must complete two tasks." The two tasks are none other than nourishing the body and refining the self. The immortals tell us: "Internally, the mind be must awake; externally, the mind must be dead to the world." To awaken the internal mind, we must nourish the body. For the mind to be dead to the outside world, we must refine the self externally. This is what nourishing the body and refining the self externally and internally are all about.

7

Post-celestial Methods

Post-celestial methods are typically used in the early stages of foundation building. Some post-celestial methods are viable and some are not. Strictly speaking, those that are not viable are not considered post-celestial methods at all. They are too yin, too questionable, and are not worth mentioning. There are four post-celestial methods that I believe are legitimate. I shall call them the post-celestial, the pre-celestial within the post-celestial, the pre-celestial, and the pre-celestial within the pre-celestial procedures.

The post-celestial procedure works with the vapor of the yin bridge, which is the root of procreation. When this vapor stirs, it is manifested as primordial generative energy. If the practitioner can rouse it and direct it into the internal cauldron, generative energy will be transmuted into vital energy, and the gates and the One cavity will open.

The procedure of the pre-celestial within the post-celestial is concerned with routing the vapor to the five viscera, where it will spread to bathe and heat the bones. Circulating through the meridians, the vapor will finally return to the dantien. When the vapor has returned to the dantien, it is time to focus the spirit, regulate the breath, and wait patiently for the mechanism of the waterwheel to move. When the waterwheel starts, you will hear a whistling sound. Immediately after this, the vapor will shoot to the top of the head. All these processes are associated with the procedure of the pre-celestial within the post-celestial.

The pre-celestial procedure requires using the sword to collect the vapor. The vapor is then harmonized, moved along the waterwheel, and finally sealed within the Yellow Pavilion. All these processes are part of the alchemical work of using the jade elixir to refine the self. When body and mind are stable and secure, you will be able to enter the chamber, approach the furnace, and seek the pre-celestial essence, which is the primordial vapor of the origin. First, take eight ounces each of the true yang and true yin that are already attracted to each other. Next, use them to erect the furnace and cauldron. Then, use the true vapor in the cauldron to entice the pre-celestial essence of your consort to emerge. This process is known as "swirling the celestial constellations." When the partner's pre-celestial essence emerges, capture it immediately. Within half an hour, a grain will materialize within the cauldron. This grain is the mother of lead and is known as the external pill.

The procedure of the pre-celestial within the pre-celestial involves using lead to create the true yang. When collected, this true vapor of yang will shine like sunlight streaming through translucent curtains. When this occurs, the generative energy within will be under control and tamed. Internal alchemists describe it as "metal returning to serve original nature" or "returning to the dantien." Now you are ready to incubate and steam the true vapor until the generative essence is secure and plentiful. Engage the yin fire and fan the yang flames daily. Preserve and protect the treasure so that it can be transformed into the golden fluid. When the precious fluid is swallowed and drawn into the five viscera, the process of the golden elixir returning to the dantien will be complete. After the elixir is ingested, the sacred fetus will be conceived. When the ten lunar months of incubation are complete, the yang spirit will appear. When the yang spirit emanates beyond your bodily shell, you will no longer be constrained by the five elements and will attain immortality.

The final stage of cultivation is called "facing the wall for nine years." It is synonymous with "refining the spirit to return to the void." When you are ready to liberate your spirit, you should sit in stillness and face an empty wall. Do not be distracted even when the myriad images of the world appear in front of you. Facing the wall does not mean simply sitting motionless in front of a blank wall. Rather, it means abiding in absolute stillness for nine years and allowing the internal pill to make nine circulations. When the pill has completed its nine circulations, you will attain transformation beyond understanding.

8

Internal and External Medicines

The internal medicine is used to recover original nature; the external medicine is used to recover original life energy. Those who want to learn how to return to their original nature and attain life must cultivate both the internal and external medicines. The internal medicine is half a pound of mercury, and the external medicine is eight ounces of lead. Before the internal medicine can be captured, the external medicine must be gathered. The external medicine is the vapor in the kidneys, and the internal medicine is the generative energy from the heart. The methods used to obtain these two medicines are post-celestial in nature.

Before original nature can be used to secure life energy, the internal medicine must be fertilized and the external medicine must be planted. In this context, the internal medicine is the mercury within the cinnabar, and the external medicine is the lead within the water. Both medicines must be cultivated after they have been gathered. In cultivating the two medicines, the external medicine is the vapor of the mother of the pill and the internal medicine is the sacred fetus. The methods referred to in this paragraph are pre-celestial in nature.

Before you can begin to work with the internal and external medicines, you must understand their meaning and function. Moreover, you must be familiar with the properties of the external and internal pills. The internal pill is the true mercury. It is the earth element of the celestial stem *ji*. Return it to the house of li and steam it, and it will be transformed into numinous cinnabar grains. The external pill is the true lead. It is the earth element of the celestial stem wu. Hidden in the house of kan, it will emerge eventually as the golden splendor. If you want to produce the internal pill, you must first use lead to control the mercury. This lead is not the lead used in the process of returning the pill to the dantien but the true fire of the partner. If you want to refine the external pill, you must use mercury to welcome the lead. This lead is not the lead responsible for creating the pill but the primordial pre-celestial vapor. Thus, the processes involved in creating the pill and returning it to the dantien are different. The creation of the pill is concerned with the activities of focusing and accumulating. Vapor from the partner is used to focus the vapor within. In this endeavor, erecting the post-celestial cauldron and the timely application of fire are essential to completing the pill. In contrast, the process of returning the pill to the dantien involves recovering something that was lost. In the return, the metal of *dui* is gathered to recover the gold of qian. In this process, the building of the pre-celestial cauldron and the copulation of yin and yang are critical.

Before the internal pill can be brought to fruition, the external pill must be created. The process of returning the pill to the dantien also requires the completion of the external pill. The internal pill is called the yin pill because it involves the emergence of mercury, and mercury is the yin within the yang. The external pill is called the yang pill because it involves the emergence of lead, and lead is the yang within the yin. The techniques of realizing the external pill require a partner to give freely, and success is dependent on joint action. The techniques of realizing the internal pill involve recovering original nature and life, and success depends on your efforts alone.

Both the production of the internal pill and the process of returning the golden elixir (the liquid form of the pill) to the dantien belong to the domain of cultivating the internal medicine, because the transformations of these substances occur internally, without external assistance. In contrast, the creation of the external pill and the golden pill belongs to the domain of cultivating the external medicine, because the transformation of these substances requires external assistance.

There is yet another meaning of the internal and external medicines. In the production of the great pill *(dadan)*, the internal and external pills are combined. In this context, the external pill is the external medicine. Sometimes the external pill refers to the transitional state when the great pill is not completely realized. In this context, the copulation of the great kan and great li, the circulation of the waterwheel, transforming vapor into fluid and directing it into the Yellow Pavilion are all part of the alchemy of compounding the external medicine. The internal pill is the internal medicine. Sometimes the internal pill refers to the state just before the great pill materializes. In this context, building the precelestial foundation, transmuting the fluid within the Crimson Palace cavity, directing the fluid to return to the Sea of Vapor (qihai), and transforming fluid into vapor are all part of the alchemy of compounding the internal medicine. The practice of cultivating clarity and stillness is integral to the realization of both the internal and external medicines. I hope you now have a better idea of the meanings of the two medicines.

9

Types of Medicines

Different types of medicines are used in the pre- and post-celestial procedures.

First, post-celestial kan and li are used to build the foundation of the pill, while pre-celestial kan and li are used to strengthen the foundation of the pill. Second, post-celestial lead and mercury are used in creating the lesser pill, and mercury and pre-celestial lead are used in the return of the great pill to the dantien. The return of the great pill to the dantien is the highest level of cultivation, which includes refining the self for three years to recover original nature and facing the wall for nine years. Third, post-celestial kan and li are involved in facilitating the copulation of the primordial spirit and primordial vapor, building the foundation of the pill, and realizing the lesser medicine. In contrast, pre-celestial kan and li are involved in facilitating the copulation of the true yin and true yang, strengthening the foundation of the pill, and realizing the greater medicine. Fourth, post-celestial lead and mercury are heated in the golden cauldron to create the external medicine called lead. When the waterwheel turns, the flow of the pearl drops can be controlled. These drops are none other than the internal mercury. When lead and mercury embrace, the lesser pill will emerge. Pre-celestial lead and mercury are the essences of yin and yang that combine to produce the earth element of the celestial stem wu. The earth of wu is the external lead. When the fire stops, the earth of wu will merge with the earth of the celestial stem ji. The earth of ji is the internal mercury. When external lead and internal mercury are introduced to each other, the great pill will return to the dantien.

When the lesser pill is heated and refined, the belly will be full and you will feel as if intoxicated. Engage the microcosmic circulation during the time of zi and wu, and gather and accumulate gradually. When lead and mercury follow your command, the yin cinnabar grains will materialize. After the great pill has coagulated and the fire in the furnace has become red-hot, add the fire of the external furnace, increasing and decreasing the heat when necessary. In time, the lead will dry, the mercury will appear, and the yang cinnabar grains will materialize.

In refining the self and recovering original nature, you need to use the yin cinnabar grains to produce the yang cinnabar grains. Internally, you must preserve generative energy and strengthen vital energy. Externally, you must forget the self in the midst of worldly dust. Only in this way can body and mind be secure and safe. The three years of incubation is involved with the production of the yang cinnabar grains. The nine years of facing the wall is concerned with recovering life, nourishing the yang cinnabar grains, circulating the pill nine times, and returning it to the dantien. When everything is dissolved and extinguished in stillness, the primordial spirit will be able to take on corporeal forms in endless transformations.

10

Nourishing the Three Substances

The *Mind Seal Classic (Xinyinqing)* states that there are three kinds of precious medicines—generative, vital, and spirit energies—and that they should be cultivated and treasured. I will now discuss their creation, transmutation, and relationships.

In the process of reverse movement, generative energy is transmuted into vital energy, and vital energy is transmuted into spirit energy. In the process of forward movement, spirit energy creates vital energy, and vital energy creates generative energy. Why do we need to practice the technique of reverse movement? It is because for most people primordial energy begins to dissipate at puberty. When primordial energy leaks out, the generative, vital, and spirit energies will lose their pre-celestial qualities and de-grade into their post-celestial state. As a result, the typical person will be unable to harness and use the energies in their primordial form. When you cannot gather the energies in their primordial state, you need to get them from a partner. When you absorb en-ergy from a partner, the method of reversal is used. To transmute generative energy into vital energy, we take the generative energy from the yin bridge, reverse its flow, direct it into the Purple Pavil-ion, and refine it. Only then can generative energy be transmuted into vapor. To transmute vital energy into spirit, we take the vapor in the yang furnace, reverse its flow, direct it into the Yellow Pavil-ion, and refine it. Only then can vapor (vital energy) be trans-muted into spirit. The method of reversal starts with gathering generative energy, while the method of forward movement starts with focusing the spirit.

Focusing the spirit is not only important in the method of forward movement, it is also integral to using the method of reversal to cultivate primordial generative energy. When spirit is focused, vapor will gather. When vapor gathers, generative energy will be created. When spirit and vapor copulate, the pre-celestial generative energy will emerge. This generative energy is the water of the celestial numeric one. It is the celestial stem ren contained in kan and is often referred to as the mother vapor or the external generative energy. Just as the mother vapor is used to conceive the child vapor, the external generative energy is used to replenish internal generative energy. The child vapor is the vapor of the heart, while the internal generative energy is the generative essence of the heart. The post-celestial techniques of preserving and nourishing life energy typically begin outside and work gradually inside. This is because the external medicine must be cultivated before it can be turned into internal medicine.

It is also possible for spirit energy to be transmuted into generative energy and generative energy to be transmuted into vapor. These processes involve transmuting the vapor into fluid in the Crimson Palace cavity and activating the waterwheel. Additionally, vapor can be used to create generative energy, and generative energy can be used to create spirit. These processes are described as white clouds rising and sweet nectar descending, and they are part of the procedure of extracting the yang from kan to replenish the yin of li.

Master Tao once said, "If you understand the internal but not the external, you won't be able to penetrate the gates and the One cavity. If you practice the methods of the external but neglect the internal, you won't be able to secure the roots." I hope practitioners now understand how generative, vital, and spirit energies can preserve, nourish, and create each other mutually in the most subtle ways.

The Five Stages of Refining

In the alchemical classics, the refining of generative, vital, and spirit energies is divided into three stages. In practice, however, more than three stages are involved. If you don't follow the steps accurately, the consequences can be disastrous. I will now describe these steps for you.

The first stage involves refining generative energy. Here, we take the cauldron and join it with the primordial yellow. After these two have interacted with each other, the golden raven will emerge and fly upward. This is the process of transmuting generative energy into vital energy.

The second stage involves understanding the meaning of zi and wu and knowing how to extract the yang from dui to replenish the yin in li. This is the process of transmuting vital energy into spirit energy. The alchemical work concerned with building the foundation and returning the great pill to the dantien is similar. The two processes differ only in the required medicines and the type of furnace and cauldron.

The third stage involves refining the spirit. This stage can be subdivided into three steps. First, we refine the spirit to recover original nature; next, we refine the spirit to recover original life; finally, we refine the spirit to return to the void. The process of refining the spirit to recover original nature concerns using the jade elixir to refine the self. Lead is used to tame mercury in order to complete the foundation of the pill. Internally, the true fire must burn constantly. Externally, extracting and replenishing must occur in the hours of zi and wu. Collection and accumulation must be gradual, and mercury must be heated until it is transformed into grains of yin cinnabar.

The process of refining the spirit to recover original life concerns using the golden elixir to refine the bodily form. Lead is returned home to tame mercury in order to conceive the fetus. Internally, the fire must be heated until it becomes red-hot. Externally, the principles of yin and yang must be applied jointly. The amount of fire and heat must be increased and decreased according to a daily schedule. Finally, when moisture is completely squeezed out of the mercury, the grains of yang cinnabar will materialize.

The processes of refining the spirit to return to the void to merge with the Tao concern moving the spirit to the Upper Court, sitting in stillness, emptying the mind, and merging with the Great Void. When the light within emanates and shines on thousands of myriad worlds, the Diamond Body will be realized. As rays of light from the dharmic seed spread in all directions, multiple bodily forms will appear and life energy will be inexhaustible. Like countless children and grandchildren, these emanations of the spirit will help you complete the final alchemical transformation. When you return to the Three Clear Realms, the Tao in you will be carried by your descendants for nine generations.

12

The Stages of Creating the Medicine

The creation of the medicine is divided into three stages. In the first stage, the medicinal substances emerge from the nonsubstantial. In the next stage, these substantive entities become nonsubstantive. In the final stage, substances are created again, this time from nothingness.

When we talk about substances that emerge from the nonsubstantial, we are referring to post-celestial fire and lead. Although these two originate from the outside, they have no form and no substantive nature. The vapor of metal is born from that which has no form or substance. When we talk about substantive entities returning to a nonsubstantive state, we are referring to the process of escorting the substances to their western homeland. Although the substances originate from the inside, they will become formless when they are returned to their original home. When we talk about creating substance from nothingness, we are referring to the emergence of the precious entity from dui. This entity is the one pre-celestial vapor born from the void. Internal alchemists describe the phenomenon of substance arising from nothingness in this way: "Out of the formless arises the subtle form, and out of nonsubstance arises the numinous substance." Look for this mysterious substance in the hours of zi and wu, and compound them in the hours of zi (11 P.M.–1 A.M.), wu (11 A.M.–1 P.M.), mao (5–7 A.M.), and you (5–7 P.M.). When the compounding is complete, the golden pill will materialize and the fetus will be conceived.

After the fetus has been incubated and nourished for the required period of time, the yang spirit will appear.

People nowadays don't know how substances can emerge from the nonsubstantial, how substances can return to the state of the nonsubstantial, and how substances can be created out of nothingness. These three processes are closely related. It is for this reason that I have described and explained them together.

13

The Three Stages of Applying the Medicines

Medicine is applied in three stages. First, the external medicine is gathered and used to manufacture the internal medicine. Next, the internal medicine is used to cultivate the external medicine. Finally, the external medicine is ingested and merged with the internal medicine.

Gathering the external medicine to manufacture the internal medicine is part of building the foundation to refine the self. Here, external medicine is used to refine the lesser medicine; this process occurs during the transmutation of generative into vital energy. Using the internal medicine to cultivate the external medicine is part of the procedure of joining the sky and earth in the cauldron. Here, the internal medicine is the true mercury, and it is used to sow the seed of the generative essence. Ingesting the external medicine and merging it with the internal medicine is concerned with using lead to tame mercury and forging the relationship between the mother and the child. Here, the external medicine is known as the great medicine. Accumulate sufficient amounts of it and you will feel intoxicated. Keep it secure within and you will never age. Incubate it and it will become the sacred fetus. When the processes of nourishing and steaming are complete, you will become immortal. Like the great sage, you can now retire, because your work is complete.

Someone asked the sage Duanyang, "The great teacher Shang-yang once said that the internal medicine is used to recover original mind in order to complete the pill, and the external medicine is used to recover original life in order to complete the circuit of returning the pill to the dantien. Given this, it would seem that the practitioner must cultivate the internal medicine before the external medicine. Why does the sage Yingzhan disagree and say that the external medicine must be cultivated first?"

Duanyang replied, "There is no disagreement between the two teachers. You have confused the post-celestial external medicine with the pre-celestial external medicine. Both the external and internal medicines are said to reside in the celestial stem gui. The names are similar, but they refer to two different entities. If you are stuck in semantics, you will misunderstand the true meaning. This misunderstanding occurs when people do not receive guidance from a teacher. It is for this reason that I want to explain the differences between the different kinds of medicine."

14

Two Kinds of Cinnabar Grains

To complete the post-celestial path, we need to use lead to tame mercury and manufacture the cinnabar grains. This cinnabar grain is the treasure attained by the return of the numeric seven to the dantien. Clear and uncontaminated, these grains are the key to the process of the lesser return of the pill to the dantien.

To complete the pre-celestial path, we need to extract lead to replenish mercury and manufacture another kind of cinnabar grain. This cinnabar grain is the treasure attained by circulating the numeric nine and returning it to the dantien. Attaining this kind of cinnabar grain is the key to the process of the greater return of the pill to the dantien. When both kinds of cinnabar grains are attained and returned to the dantien, the body will be bathed in a golden light.

15

Spirit, Vapor, Original Nature, and Life

The post-celestial path works with spirit and vapor; the pre-celestial path works with original nature and life. Original nature and life are closely related to spirit and vapor respectively. This is why the text *Adding the Medicine (Ruyaojing)* states: "Original nature and life are like and yet unlike spirit and vapor. Water and lead come from the same home and originate from the same substance." Experienced practitioners understand this well. They know that spirit and vapor are involved in completing the post-celestial path, while original nature and life are involved in completing the pre-celestial path.

Before their manifestation, original nature and life are one. Understanding this is the key to realizing original nature and recovering life. *Understanding Reality* states: "Although the two are given different names, they originate from the same source. Subtle and mysterious, the two are the key to everything." What we call life comes from the same source as original nature. Likewise, what we call lead comes from the same source as mercury. This is what is meant by "the original home of water and lead are one and the same." The *Tao Te Ching* says: "Seek it in action and you will see the subtleties; seek it in nonaction and you will see the One cavity." The secret workings of the subtle mysteries can be summed up by this statement: In absolute stillness and in the absence of desire you will see the subtleties. This absolute stillness is necessary for stabilizing original nature. When it is time for movement to occur, the one primordial vapor of the origin will emerge from the void and the One cavity will materialize. Original nature and primordial vapor both originate from the taiji. In nothingness, we see the subtleties of original nature and attain the One Mystery. In existence, we experience the primordial vapor of the One cavity and will also attain the One Mystery. The two mysteries are subtle beyond subtleties. This is why where there is original nature there will also be life.

Original nature comes from heaven, and life emerges with original nature. Heaven uses vapor to create all things, and the myriad things grow and mature according to the principles of heaven. Before their manifestation, life and original nature are joined. This is the meaning of the phrase "original nature is life." Following the principles of creation, humankind procreates and uses the vapor to generate another human being. In this process, original nature is used to produce a life.

How can life be regained by recovering original nature? In the path of mortals, procreation is possible because of the existence of vapor; in the path of immortality, the creation of vapor is possible because of the principles of procreation. Vapor that is responsible for procreation is heavy and is capable of warming, steaming, and intoxicating. When a body receives this vapor, a human fetus is formed. When the vapor takes on the form of a fetus, it is heavy and will stay in its container, the womb. The vapor that emerges according to the principles of procreation is the one primordial true vapor of the origin, and it too is heavy. When yin receives the light of yang, lead is planted within the lead, and the one yang is born. If the vapor is not heavy, it will not sink into the navel. If the vapor of procreation does not sink, the one true lead (vapor) will not emerge. Without the lead vapor, the golden elixir cannot be circulated and returned to the dantien. Now that you understand the value of the lead (vapor), you should cultivate and treasure it.

16

The Meaning of Pre-celestial

Pre-celestial means above and beyond post-celestial. Most primal and present at the beginning of all things, it is the origin of all existence and the ruler of the one undifferentiated vapor.

There are several meanings of "pre-celestial." First, by pre-celestial, we mean that which gives birth to the sky. This pre-celestial existed before the sky emerged and is the creator of sky and earth. Within this pre-celestial is vapor, and this vapor is part of the undifferentiated oneness that was originally called the Great Nothingness.

Second, by pre-celestial, we refer to that which originates from the sky. This pre-celestial gives birth to humankind and all things. Capable of incubating and providing warmth, its structure is hidden in the Great Void. Within this pre-celestial is also vapor, and this vapor existed before humans were born and things were created.

Third, by pre-celestial, we mean that which can help us to attain immortality or enlightenment. Within this pre-celestial is also vapor, and this vapor comes from the absolute nothingness called the *taiyi* (Great Beginning). When we attain this vapor, the golden pill will materialize. Other names for this vapor are the ancestral, the beginning, and the true vapor.

Thus, there are three forms of pre-celestial: that which gives birth to the sky, that which originates from the sky, and that which is the spark of enlightenment. The ancient internal alchemical classics talk only about the pre-celestial vapor that gives birth to sky and earth and the vapor that creates humankind and all things. I tell you now that there is also a pre-celestial vapor that gives birth to the immortal and the Buddha within.

Someone asked the sage Duanyang about the pre-celestial that gives birth to the sky and the earth. He replied: "This pre-celestial is born from the Great Ultimate. The ancients called it the creator of all things. It cannot be named, so for convenience we call it the Tao. This vapor is the ancestor of the ten thousand forms and the origin of the two great essences (yin and yang). It has no form, no sound, and no smell. When it first emerges, it is subtle and elusive and is untouched by the five elements. Existing yet not existing, appearing yet hidden, it is the one natural vapor. When the clear and muddy are separated, the mysterious yellow is born. When the mysterious yellow merges, qian and kun will occupy their positions, and sky and earth are differentiated."

Someone asked about the pre-celestial that gives birth to humankind and all things.

Duanyang replied, "This pre-celestial is the ruler of the sky and the earth. It is one and yet three, and three and yet one. When it is one, it is the primordial vapor. When manifested as three entities, they are the generative, vital, and spirit energies. The one and the three are that which create and nourish all things. Generative energy is the procreative essence of the numerics two and five. Vital energy is the breath of yin and yang. Spirit energy is the numinous spirit of the void. The spirit of the void interacts with the breath of yin and yang, and the breath of yin and yang in conjunction with the numerics two and five of the generative energy give birth to the numinous vapor. When vapor is numinous, the spirit will be numinous. When the spirit is numinous, vapor and its workings will be subtle and wondrous. When vapor is subtle, generative energy will swirl up and down in synchrony with the vapor. The essence and the spirit of the sky and the earth are embodied in this vapor. When humans receive this vapor, a fetus is conceived. Although this vapor originates from the primordial sky, it can be clear or muddy, hard or soft. When hardness is manifested, males are conceived. When softness is manifested, females are conceived. Those who are endowed with clear vapor will be intelligent, and those who receive muddy vapor will be dull-witted. Before our father and mother copulated, this vapor was stored in a cavity. When our birth parents interacted sexually, this vapor moved to the orifices. When generative essence and blood merge, the fetus is conceived. However, after conception, the vapor remains in the womb. Enclosed within the womb, the spirit is merged with vapor and therefore does not have a separate identity. Generative energy also does not have a separate identity because it too is a part of the vapor. When the vapor is enclosed inside the womb, generative essence is locked within and cannot dissipate. The energies sealed within the womb are the primordial generative, vital, and spirit energies. If you are destined to receive instructions from a teacher and cultivate this primordial energy before puberty, you will be able to attain immortality easily.

"There are also three pre-celestial substances called the true vapor, true spirit, and true generative essence. These three entities are required for compounding the pill. Practitioners who don't understand the true workings of these three substances will not know how to recover the precious treasure. The ancient sages said: 'The energy that can be seen is that which cannot be used, and the energy that can be used is that which cannot be seen.' The essence of these energies will appear when the practitioner is able to attain absolute emptiness and stillness. These energies are created from nothingness, and in their original state they are merged together. The true spirit is the nonspirit of spirit; the true generative essence is the purest manifestation of generative energy; and the true vapor is the one true primordial vapor. They are three manifestations of the one primordial substance.

"The nonspirit of spirit is the absolute spirit; it is the original nature of the dragon. The purest essence of procreation is the absolute generative energy; it is the feelings of the tiger. Both are manifestations of the same entity. The one true vapor is the true lead that allows us to recover life. Merged with the original nature of the dragon and the feelings of the tiger, it is called the mother of the pill. The true vapor is also called the true One. If you attain the true One, the three monsters (that attack the three energies) and five thieves (that steal the five senses) will vanish, and eternal spring will rule in the thirty-six palaces. This vapor cannot be equated with the generative, vital, and spirit energies that give birth to a human, nor can it be compared with the post-celestial generative, vital, and spirit energies.

"In the post-celestial domain, the breath we inhale and exhale, the spirit that thinks and perceives, and the procreative energy that is aroused sexually are things that can be seen and felt. They emerge after our bodies came into existence. This is why it is said that they are post-celestial in nature. When a fetus is conceived in the womb, it knows only the primordial vapor, because there is no contact with the world outside. When the ten lunar months of conception are complete, the fetus leaves the mother's womb. The orifices open, and the infant now uses its mouth and nostrils to breathe, thus activating the mundane breath. With time, the spirit becomes the thinking mind. Together with the external breath, the mind takes control of the home of the spirit. This thinking mind is the seed that dooms us to reincarnation and suffering. It is first to emerge when we are born and first to leave when we die. Shedding the old shell, it will take up residence in a new shell after forty-nine days. Thus, the moment the infant drops out of its mother's womb, it is destined for suffering and reincarnation. As the infant becomes a youth, the scheming and conceptualizing mind will become dominant, and original mind will recede. With the onset of puberty, sexual desire will strangle the body, and the primordial vapor will dissipate daily. As the youth becomes an adult, he or she will depend more and more on the mundane breath to sustain life. This is something sad and lamentable.

"We are not the ruler of post-celestial generative energy. We cannot command it to come when we are born, and we cannot take it with us when we die. The post-celestial generative energy owes its existence to the natural growth of primordial vapor when we were young. At fifteen, yang reaches its height and yin emerges. From then on, yang will wane and yin will wax strong. With the onset of puberty and the arousal of sexual feelings, the one undifferentiated vapor is transformed into procreative energy. If there is no arousal, however, the transformation will not occur.

Procreative energy is forced to emerge only when there is sexual desire. When sexual feelings are present, vapor will be transformed into blood. If vapor and blood are weak and unstable, sexual arousal can also occur in dreams and sleep. Consequently, the vapor in the cavities of the kidneys cannot be conserved. The generative energy we are referring to here is the procreative energy that is aroused and expelled during sexual intercourse.

"It is important for students to practice diligently so that they can recover their pre-celestial existence, leave the post-celestial existence behind, and attain the highest medicine. Build the foundation and refine the body. Do not look for shortcuts. Focus on refining the primordial generative energy so that it can be transmuted into primordial vital energy. Refine the vital energy so that it can give birth to the true lead. Finally, use the pre-celestial substance that you have attained to rebuild and recover the eight ounces of the post-celestial. When you have accomplished all these things, you will be able to enter the ultimate pre-celestial realm."

17

Spirit, Vital, and Generative Energies

The *Mind Seal Classic* states: "There are three precious medicines: spirit, vital, and generative energies." These three wondrous substances are the key to cultivating the pill. Of highest quality are the primordial spirit, primordial vapor, and primordial generative essence. Next are the true generative, vital, and spirit energies.

What is meant by "primordial"? By primordial, we mean pre-celestial. The primordial energy is often called the pre-celestial energy because it is born in the Royal Descent *(huangjiang)* cavity; it is the primal celestial energy of youth before puberty. The true pre-celestial energy originates in the Great Tao. However, with growth and maturity, the true pre-celestial energy is transformed into primal human energy, which is the essence of procreation in the adult body. If you missed the chance to cultivate the primal celestial energy of youth, you'll need to cultivate the primal human energy instead.

A student asked, "It appears that the primal celestial energy is very important in cultivating the Tao. Can you please tell me more about it?"

Duanyangzi replied, "The primal celestial energy is the yin and yang and the five elements that give birth to humankind and all things. Vapor gives form to life, and the principles of growth allow life to mature. The vapor that gives birth to life is called the primordial vapor. Before our father and mother copulated, this vapor was stored within their bodies. During sexual intercourse, the vapor descended to the orifices. The Confucians describe this process as 'sky giving birth to humans, and with birth the laws of growth follow.' This vapor is numinous. Because it is numinous, it embodies the spirit. This spirit is the primordial spirit. The numinous vapor is also pure and clear. Because it is pure and clear, it embodies the essence of generative energy. This essence is none other than the primordial generative essence.

"Inside the mother's womb, there is only primordial vapor. Because the fetus does not inhale and exhale external air, post-celestial breath is absent. As the fetus approaches its time of birth, its mouth and nostrils become fully developed. The fetus now breathes in synchrony with the mother's inhalation and exhalation, taking in the great harmonious vapor of the sky and the earth. However, at the same time, the yin spirit of reincarnation begins to enter with each breath. When the infant comes into contact with both post-celestial spirit and breath, it is ready to tumble out of the mother's womb. Fortunately for the infant, it has no faculty of speech, thought, emotion, or desire. The primordial vapor still swirls within its body because concepts, reason, and anxiety have not emerged. Thus, although the yin spirit is present, it is unable (for the time being) to control the infant's existence. Consequently, primordial vapor and primordial spirit can still work together to nourish the body.

"At puberty, the child's spirit and vapor will reach their height of development. As yang reaches its extreme, yin will emerge. Following this principle, primordial vapor is transformed into sexual generative energy. With the onset of puberty, the fires of desire are ignited, and the yin spirit will begin to control both mind and body. Therefore, it is best if you can meet a teacher and begin your cultivation before puberty. If you possess the primordial pre-celestial body, all you'll need to do to attain the Tao is to cultivate clarity and stillness. With continued practice, you can become a celestial immortal in no time. If you wait until post-celestial existence has taken hold, you will no longer possess the pre-celestial body. As a result, you won't be able to take the short path to immortality. The sages tell us that it is easy for young practitioners to cultivate pre-celestial energy because the body and mind of a youth are closest to those of an immortal. Some would even equate a child with an immortal.

"Sky and earth give birth to humankind, establishing the celestial principles and fostering the celestial virtues. If you can focus and keep the celestial within, you will be able to attain great transformations. Otherwise, it will be hard for you to attain immortality. Adults who have taken the forward path of procreation will need to practice the method of reversal to give birth to the immortal fetus. This is how human primordial energy works: On the one hand, it creates all things and cannot be exhausted; on the other hand, it is bounded by sky and earth and does not go beyond their limits. If you understand the properties of the generative, vital, and spirit energies, the path of immortality will be open to you."

Someone asked, "What is the difference between the primordial spirit and the true spirit?"

Duanyangzi answered, "The primordial spirit is undifferentiated and ephemeral; the true spirit is clear and bright. The former hides within the chaos and is without light; the latter is tempered and refined. The Confucians say that clear thinking comes from a peaceful and still mind. The Buddhists say that deep intuition comes from attaining ultimate wisdom (prajna). The Taoists say that intelligent wisdom is born from harmony and stillness. They all refer to the subtle workings of the true spirit.

"The primordial spirit is unthinking and unknowing; the conceptual mind knows and thinks too much; the true spirit thinks and acts, but its intelligence is round and bright. Young practitioners possess the pre-celestial body; if they cultivate clarity and stillness, they'll attain the true spirit. This is why the path of single practice is best suited for youthful practitioners. Adult and aging practitioners have lost their pre-celestial body; therefore, they must not only cultivate clarity and stillness but also renew and refine the body before they can attain the true spirit. This is why the path of paired practice is best suited for adult and aging practitioners."

Someone else asked, "What is the difference between primordial generative essence and true generative energy?"

Duanyangzi replied, "The primordial generative essence is within us; the true generative energy is in the other (the partner). The vapor of the generative essence is stored in the Crimson Palace cavity. When sufficient amounts of this vapor are accumulated, the numinous liquid will emerge. The true generative energy in the partner is the strong and thrusting vapor of the Radiant Pool *(huachi)* cavity. It is what *Understanding Reality* referred to as freshly produced generative blood. On the fifteenth day of the eighth lunar month, when the full moon is bright, the vapor of metal will be at its height of production. Add to this the numerics two and eight (age sixteen), and the power of the true generative energy will be like a tidal wave. If you understand the properties of this true generative energy and know how to absorb it at the right time, your path to immortality will be shortened, because this substance is not trivial."

Another student asked, "What is the difference between primordial vapor and true vital energy?"

Duanyangzi said, "The primordial vapor is what the infant has received from the celestial realm. It is the vapor that gives birth to its form and nourishes its body. The true vital energy is the ancestor of the great beginning of pre-celestial existence and is born of the void. To attain it, you must receive personal instruction from a teacher on how to erect the cauldron of qian and kun, how to harmonize the true dragon and true tiger, and how to join together the true yin and true yang. Apply these techniques at the right time, and the mother of lead will materialize. The yang that emerges from the lead is the true vapor.

"Heaven uses the primordial vapor to create humankind; the Tao uses the true vapor to create immortals and bodhisattvas. The human primordial technique used in refining the vapor has the power to capture the transforming power of the sky and the earth. This technique is not easy to learn."

Several students asked Duanyangzi about the difference between the primordial celestial and the primordial human methods.

Duanyangzi told them: "Original nature is celestial will and destiny. The principles of procreation emerge from the One vapor. The original technique of creating generative energy from vapor is pre-celestial in nature. However, this technique is not viable for people who have lost their pre-celestial body. In order to recover original nature and attain life, older practitioners will need to use techniques derived from the principles of procreation. Creating generative energy this way is part of the primordial human method.

"High virtue follows the principles of nonaction and cannot be forced. Only those of high virtue can walk the primordial celestial path and practice single cultivation in clarity and stillness. Lesser virtue follows the principles of function and inexhaustible use. Those of lesser virtue must walk the primordial human path and practice the method of reversal. Those who embody high virtue are favored by heaven: They have been granted the opportunity to practice single cultivation. The goal of their practice is to refine the primordial vapor and primordial spirit into their purest forms by cultivating clarity and stillness. Only those who possess high virtue can practice single cultivation and take advantage of the workings of the primordial celestial. If you have not broken your pre-celestial body when you begin your cultivation, you will be very close to primordial celestial existence.

"The majority of people, however, belong to the realm of lesser virtue; therefore, they must take the primordial human path and learn the method of reversal. They need to join together the yin and yang pills and refine them before they can enter the great nothingness and Great Void. The primordial human path focuses on recovering the pristine body and is most suitable for those who possess only the lesser virtue. It is called the primordial human path because the source (of energy) lies in another human.

"In the domain of high virtue, original nature and life nourish each other mutually. In the world of lesser virtue, original nature and life must both be recovered jointly by using the vapor to refine the mind and the mind to temper the body. Heaven uses the vapor of yin and yang and the five elements to create humankind. In the same manner, when humans receive the one true vapor of the primal beginning, they can use it to create the immortal fetus. The method of transforming the sky and earth within is no different from heaven's way of creation."

18

Further Discussion on Generative, Vital, and Spirit Energies

In the domain of high virtue, generative, vital, and spirit energies are called the primordial energies. Primordial energy is a great gift from heaven, and those who possess it will not need to obtain it from another person. This is because the primordial energy is the celestial primordial vapor. In the domain of low virtue, generative, vital, and spirit energies are called the true energies. If you cannot produce these energies within, you will need to gather them from another. Because true energy is collected from another person, we call it the human primordial vapor.

Within the primordial human path, there are several methods of gathering the primordial energies and penetrating the secret workings. When we take the primordial human path to return to celestial primordial existence, we need to gather the primordial generative energy to replenish the primordial vital energy, refine the primordial vital energy to nourish the primordial spirit, and refine the primordial spirit to attain the true spirit. Once you have accomplished these processes, the alchemical work of the post-celestial path will be complete. From here on, the true spirit will be used to produce the true vital energy, and the true vital energy will be used to produce the true generative energy. When the true generative energy is transformed into the true lead, the alchemical work of the pre-celestial path will be complete. At this time, you will be able to return to the origin, embrace the primordial, and hold on to the One. Once you have accomplished these transformations, your practice will be similar to that of the path of high virtue.

However, if those in the domain of low virtue cannot reach the realm of stillness and if those in the domain of high virtue do not understand the subtleties of nonaction, neither will be able to attain celestial primordial existence and become a celestial immortal.

19

The Forward and Reverse Paths of Cultivating Original Nature and Life

There are two ways of cultivating original nature and life: the forward path and the reverse path. The forward path is decreed by celestial destiny. In this path, original nature and life have always been one. The reverse path is tied to human existence. In this path, we take the two and combine them to become one. When original nature and life are not separated, vapor is produced according to the principles of creation. When vapor and the principles of creation are joined, they become original nature and life. When the two are separated, they must be combined to become one. Water must be used to extinguish fire, and when water and fire interact, original nature and life will be recovered.

In the forward path, celestial will is embodied in original nature, and original nature is joined with life. When Mencius spoke of the body having celestial nature, he was equating the body with original life. Where there is body, there is original nature. The original nature of goodness is a manifestation of life. Attain original nature and you will recover life. In the reverse path, we recover life in order to attain original nature. This requires using the sacred fire within to plant the precious seed of life. This path is possible because original nature embodies both spirit and life, and because spirit and life, being part of the sacred light of original nature, can resonate with each other.

Those who belong to the domain of high virtue are able to take the forward path. Using the method of single practice, they can conceive the immortal fetus by cultivating clarity and stillness. This is what is meant by using celestial destiny to complete human destiny. Those who belong to the domain of low virtue, however, must take the reverse path and conceive the sacred fetus using the method of paired practice. Students of the Tao should be clear about what is required by these two different paths.

20

The One Cavity of the Mysterious Gate

The One cavity of the Mysterious Gate is born from the void. It does not reside in the five viscera, the six bowels, or the muscles and bones. I will now tell you why this cavity is called the Mysterious Gate. The One cavity is the gate to the secret, mysterious, and subtle workings of the Tao. It is the cavity where all the techniques converge into one method. There is no other cavity like it.

The One cavity can be described as that which is in the middle. By middle, we mean that it is between the upper and lower and yet not between the upper and lower. There is a "dead" cavity and a "live" cavity. A dead cavity is one that is tied to a location in the body, such as the Yellow Pavilion or the lower dantien. A live cavity is one that emerges when the spirit is focused and vapor is gathered. The One cavity, or the Mysterious Gate, is a live cavity. This One cavity is born out of nothingness. It is numinous, and its workings are truly subtle and mysterious. Those who understand the workings of the One cavity do not talk about it casually.

21

Further Discussion on the Mysterious Gate

The Mysterious Gate glows with a numinous light that is the result of spirit and vapor copulating. When the gate first emerges, its light is unstable and its existence is elusive. This is because when spirit and vapor are first introduced to each other, they do not join together comfortably. It is only when spirit and vapor are in full embrace that the workings of the Mysterious Gate are fully realized. For spirit and vapor to embrace, the active mind must be dead. When the active mind is dead, the spirit will not stray. When spirit does not stray, duality of self and other will dissolve, and ghosts and spirits will be unable to predict your actions. Tumbling and swirling in the undifferentiated chaos, you are now at one with the wondrous mystery. When you reach this state of existence, you will be capable of transformations beyond name and imagination. No wonder people describe the Mysterious Gate in many ways. The ancient sages never talked about it openly. Only those whose "point of exit" on top of their head is opened and who have received the precepts will know the secret workings of the Mysterious Gate. Adept practitioners say that the One cavity is not located in the heart nor the kidneys, and, as I have mentioned, it should not be equated with the Yellow Pavilion cavity or the lower dantien. I have gone beyond what the ancient ones have said about this cavity, hoping that those who have attained it will appreciate its workings.

22

The Cavity with Two Openings

The alchemical texts tell us that the One cavity has two openings and is empty in the center. This is why it is called the cavity with dual openings. My teacher told me that the One cavity emerges when mouth is linked with mouth and opening is connected to opening. These linkages are located where the ren and du meridians meet. Here, yin and yang interact, and the raven and rabbit play.

Special procedures have been designed to open the dual orifices of the One cavity. These procedures involve the method of action and are most subtle. The *Triplex Unity* states: "When the upper end is closed, the cavity comes into being; when the lower end is closed, it does not exist. The upper end must be absolutely empty because the virtuous spirit resides on top. To activate the two openings, the vapor of metal is required." These statements capture the essence of the method of activating the two openings. By upper and lower, we mean sky and earth. By closing, we mean completing the circuit when the two openings are joined. By existing and nonexisting, we refer to the characteristics of the subtle cavity. This is how the form and qualities of the One cavity are typically described.

Both upper and lower ends are hidden in the cavity. As it is existing yet not existing, everything is enclosed within it. In absolute emptiness and stillness, sky and earth will join and we will experience the cavity's subtleties. These subtleties, however, cannot be named; we can only say that somehow they exist. The internal alchemists describe this joining as "the ephemeral merging of the generative energies" and "activating the female generative power within the generative fluid." The cavity will emerge only in a state of nothingness. It is said that the cavity of the absolute void has a structure and is yet without structure. It is also said that the cavity originates from nothingness because a substance that exists has returned to nonexistence.

While it is said that the upper end should be empty, this does not mean that there is nothing there. Rather, it means that what is there has neither structure nor form. This formless entity is the pre-celestial true lead. Try to encounter it from the front and you won't be able see its head. Follow it from behind and you won't see its tail. When internal alchemists talk about "the upper part being served by stillness," they are referring to using nothingness to generate existence. What do we mean by serving? And whom are we serving? We serve the virtuous spirit with emptiness, and when the service is complete, the vapor will return naturally. The biggest problem facing practitioners is when there is no virtuous spirit above. By above, we mean above the Yellow Pavilion; by virtue, we mean humility and softness. This is summed up aptly by a phrase from the *Triplex Unity:* "The test of whether the Tao is attained and whether the pivot of virtue exists lies in the application of softness."

Apply the principles of the Tao when you are in absolute emptiness. Use virtue to attain the lead. Virtue belongs to the path of action; the Tao belongs to the path of nonaction. The two openings of the One cavity make up the gate of the Mysterious Female. It is within the One cavity that the golden pill is born. If you know how to gather the precious substance into the dual openings of the One cavity, the two gates will open and the metal will return home to merge with original nature. This is the process of "returning the pill to the dantien," and the key to this process lies in the production of the vapor of metal, which in turn requires the joint activities of gathering and absorbing.

23

The Foundation of the Mysterious Female

Whether cultivating the great pill or the lesser pill, practitioners of internal alchemy must nourish the valley spirit in stillness and build its foundation. The valley spirit is the pre-celestial numinous void. It is also our original nature.

The valley spirit is nourished inside the Mysterious Female. The sage Shangyang said, "The Mysterious Female is made of two entities. Without them, all things cannot be created." The two entities are sky, which we name Mysterious, and earth, which we name Female. They are equivalent to the father and mother trigrams qian and kun.

The cavity known as the Mysterious Female is the source of all creation and transformation. Laozi said, "The valley spirit that does not die is the Mysterious Female." Thus, the valley spirit is synonymous with the Mysterious Female, and to attain the void of the Mysterious Female, we need to nourish the void of the valley spirit.

Much has been said about the Mysterious Female. For example, Zhang Boduan's *Four Hundred Words on the Golden Pill (Jindansibazi)* states: "The One cavity is no ordinary cavity. It is created from the joining of qian and kun, and it is called the cavity of the spirit and vapor. Within it are the essences of kan and li. Thus, the Mysterious Female nourishes not only spirit but also vapor." When spirit and vapor copulate, the cavity of the Mysterious Female emerges. Moreover, when spirit is focused and vapor is gathered, the two will copulate, and a circle formed by qian and kun in embrace will emerge. These processes are all part of the reverse path. How does the reverse path work? First, spirit needs to help the upper half focus on the lower half. In this way, the honored body of the mysterious sky will be able to initiate the humble work of the female earth. Second, the upper and lower halves must interact so that vapor and spirit can unite. This process is referred to by the *Tao Te Ching* as "copulating with the Female in the universe."

The way of the female is the way of the mysterious. This is why it is called the Mysterious Female. The Mysterious Female is made of qian and kun, hardness and softness. Thus, when the spirit is strong, vapor will also be strong. During the sacred union, you must reverse the opposing and separating forces. Let the male descend into the female, and let the spirit sink into the vapor. Engage the path of reversal, let yin and yang copulate, and allow the spirit and vapor to merge. In this way, the foundation of the Mysterious Female will be strong. If you cannot accomplish this, spirit and vapor will separate and go their own way. When spirit does not receive vapor, vapor will not be replenished. When vapor does not return to the spirit, spirit will not be nourished.

How can we get the primordial spirit to stay within? To accomplish this, we must welcome the spirit into the Crimson Palace cavity and make this cavity the command center. Knowledge, concepts, and perspective can disturb the primordial spirit. If you want to extinguish all sounds, sights, and thoughts, the Yellow Pavilion cavity must be kept empty and still. This part of the practice requires single cultivation. *Understanding Reality* states: "If you don't want the valley spirit to die, you must build the foundation of the Mysterious Female." By valley spirit, we mean absolute emptiness, which is the numinous nature of mercury. By true generative essence, we mean the clearest and freshest feelings of lead. In building the foundation of the Mysterious Female, mercury is used to attract lead, and when they are joined, the golden pill is formed. The golden chamber is the yellow bedchamber where the golden metal is stored. When the true generative essence returns to the golden chamber, the one bright pearl will never leave.

When the metal of lead copulates with the wood of mercury, a bright round pearl will be created. This bright pearl is the golden pill, and it is shaped like a large grain of rice. When metal returns to original nature, the process of returning the pill to the dantien will begin. Once the process of the return is completed, the pill will stay with you forever. This is what is meant by the mercury never leaving. Ziyang's words (in *Understanding Reality*) are very clear about this secret technique. This technique can be practiced whether you are using the pre- or post-celestial method of cultivation. Regardless of the method chosen, you must first attain the Mysterious Female. Only then can you build the foundation of the pill, realize the valley spirit, and direct the true generative essence to return to your body. Use the Mysterious Female to nourish the valley spirit, and use the valley spirit to nourish the true generative essence. When spirit is nourished by generative essence, its primal nature will be strengthened. When generative essence is nourished by the spirit, it can be transmuted into vapor. The *Triplex Unity* states: "Nourish the self within so that it becomes absolutely still and empty. When original nature rules inside, you will be able to build the roots of the foundation." To cultivate the body, we must build the proper foundation, and to build the proper foundation, we must nourish the valley spirit in stillness.

24

The Meaning of "Center"

The *Tao Te Ching* states: "Speak too much and you'll be exhausted. It is better to hold on to the center." To know the meaning of "the center" is to possess the seed of immortality and enlightenment. Otherwise, you won't know how to begin to cultivate the Tao. Worse, you'll fall into the pit of monsters with your first step and never get out.

What is the center? The center is the Mysterious Gate. The *Triplex Unity* states: "When moving and circulating, do not lose the center. Floating and swirling, always hold on to the center." Immortal Tao said, "The center is not the center of the four directions." For the Confucians, the center is the state where all things emerge. For the Taoists, it is the Mysterious Female where thoughts and desires do not exist. For the Buddhists, it is the state where there is no duality, no perspective of good and bad, and no judgment of correctness or incorrectness. In other words, the center is original nature.

To attain the wondrous subtleties of the center, we must nourish the body and refine the mind. The spirit must be focused, directed into the chamber, and returned to the dantien. Once the process of the return is completed, the sacred fetus will be transformed into spirit and eventually be liberated. It is important for beginning practitioners to understand the meaning of the center. When Immortal Wenshi asked Laozi, "What is the most important key to cultivating the Tao?" Laozi replied, "It is in planting deep roots, securing strong foundations, and focusing and holding on to oneness." I will now explain the meaning of these words.

When you first start your cultivation, you must endure tiredness in the muscles and tendons, fight the monsters of sleepiness and lethargy and distant stray thoughts, and direct the internal light into the three cavities. The three cavities are the Yellow Pavilion, the Sea of Qi (qihai), and the lower dantien. Although you are directing the light of the internal gaze into these three cavities, you should not think about the act. Let the spirit rest peacefully within, let the breath be natural, forget about everything, and dwell in nothingness. This is what the *Tao Te Ching* means by "free of desire, you can see the subtleties." When you are in a perfect state of emptiness and absolute stillness, the spirit will be focused and united with vapor. In the absence of thought and intention, a unique feeling will emerge from the center. You will experience something large materializing, but at the same time, you will know intuitively that this "something" does not exist externally. You will also feel something small emerging but know intuitively that this entity does not exist internally. This is a sign that the cavity of the Mysterious Gate has opened. When the *Tao Te Ching* says: "In thought, you can see the cavity," it is referring to what the *Triplex Unity* describes as "When the upper is closed, we call it existence; when the lower is closed, we call it nothingness." The meaning of "upper" and "lower" is encompassed in the meaning of "center." The center is where yin and yang come and go, where kan and li ascend and descend, and where upper and lower join. This is what is meant by when the upper half is empty, the lower half is closed. In the great void of the center, the only thing that circulates is the primordial vapor. This is why we say that emptiness and nothingness are the guiding principles of the subtleties. Where the lower is the master, the upper is closed. This is the state of nondifferentiation and chaos, where female generative energy is intertwined with male generative energy. In this state, existence, not nothingness, is the guiding principle of the cavity's function. When both upper and lower are closed, the two will return inside the Mysterious Female. The difference between action and nonaction lies in the subtleties of the cavity of the Mysterious Gate. By action, we refer to the subtle cavity of action and initiation. Action is the guiding principle of everything occurring in the upper and lower anvils, the yin and yang cauldrons, and the cavity of the spirit and vapor.

One of the teachers said, "Those who cultivate the Tao must first attain the subtle mystery. If you don't attain the subtle function, you won't be able to open the One cavity. If you want to open this cavity, you must ask that the Tao be shown to you." At this point, the teacher exchanged a smile with Duanyangzi.

25

Discourse on the Medicines

Shangyang said, "The medicines are produced from certain substances. There is a lesser medicine and a greater medicine. The lesser medicine is post-celestial in nature and is used to produce the pill. The greater medicine is pre-celestial in nature and is used to return the pill to the dantien. The pre-celestial medicine is without form and structure; the post-celestial medicine has both structure and function but is not substantive."

To attain the true post-celestial lead, we must abandon the celestial stem gui and obtain the celestial stem ren. The lead is the yin hidden in the yang; it is a substance that emerges from nothingness. *Understanding Reality* says: "The three primal orders and the eight trigrams originate from the celestial stem ren." The three primal orders are the primordial generative, vital, and spirit energies. Ren is born of the numeric one of sky and, in the twenty-four directions, occupies the position before (terrestrial branch) zi. Ren is the origin of the one yang. Ren and gui reside in the palace of kan. This northern water is yin in nature. Thus, the water of ren is the yang within the yin, and the water of gui is the yin within the yin. Ren and gui are celestial stems, and zi and hai are terrestrial branches. When acquiring the true lead, the celestial stems are primary and the terrestrial branches are secondary. Ren refers to the beginning of things when there were no thoughts and no attachments; it is the stillness before the movement. Zi refers to the state of knowing and perceiving; it is the final moments of stillness before the onset of movement. The yin of gui is not used. Hai has no left yin; therefore, it too is not used. This is the key to attaining the lesser medicine. (See table 1 for a list of directions, their associated trigram palaces, and their relationships to the celestial stems and terrestrial branches.)

The pre-celestial medicine is different. The pre-celestial medicine is born from kun, but its seed is sown in qian. It uses that which has substance to create nothingness and that which is in us to attain that which is in the other. When the metal of qian enters kun, it is called the metal of kun. When kun becomes kan, it is called the water in the metal. Kan resides in the north. Dui, residing in the west, is its neighbor. Metal borrows the home of dui and lives there. Thus, it is called the metal of dui. If you want to obtain this metal, do not look in qian or kun but seek it directly in dui. You won't find it in qian because qian is where the seed is sown. You won't find it in kun because kun embodies the primal origin. You won't find it in kan because although kan has yang in it, the yang is still immersed in water, where the true workings of its essence are still hidden. Search for it directly in dui, and yang will emerge and metal will appear. This is what is meant by "on the third day of the lunar month, the sun and moon both rise in the direction of *geng* (the west)." The water of kan is the source of the river, and the metal of dui is the medicine. This is what is meant by the phrase "qian, kun, kan, dui are all locations in the body." These four all participate in the process of using substance to attain nothingness and using that which is in us to attain that which is in the other. We take one single spark of yin essence of generative energy to plant the seed in the other so that the yang in the lead will be born. When the vapor of yang is aroused, we gather and return it within us, and plant the seed in the palace of the womb to conceive the immortal being. *Understanding Reality* says: "Use the other's kun to produce a bodily form, and plant it in your home through copulation." The seed planted in qian is the basis for spreading the other's seed, and planting it in the home of qian refers to that seed being nourished internally.

What I have described should explain the words of the sages Cui and Zhang: "Plant lead to obtain lead. The technique of

CHINESE COMPASS DIRECTION	WESTERN COMPASS DIRECTION	POST-CELESTIAL TRIGRAM NAME	STEM/BRANCH AND YIN/YANG AFFILIATION
ren	north	kan	yang stem
zi			yin branch
gui			yin stem
chou	northeast	gen	yin branch
gen			trigram
yin			yang branch
jia	east	zhen	yang stem
mao			yin branch
yi			yin stem
chen	southeast	xun	yin branch
xun			trigram
ji			yang branch
bing	south	li	yang stem
wu			yin branch
ding			yin stem
wei	southwest	kun	yin branch
kun			trigram
shen			yang branch
geng	west	dui	yang stem
you			yin branch
xin			yin stem
xu	northwest	qian	yin branch
qian			trigram
hai			yang branch

Table 1

The twenty-four directions of the Chinese compass, their associated equivalents in the Western compass, with the related post-celestial trigrams and the affiliated celestial stem and terrestrial branch. Each of the eight directions is associated with a trigram of the bagua, and each is subdivided into three segments. There are ten celestial stems and twelve terrestrial branches. The two celestial stems wu (which is yang) and ji (which is yin) are said to be hidden and therefore are not manifested in the twenty-four directions.

planting lead must occur between the locations of celestial stems ding and ren. Then, apply the functions of zhen and dui to take the places of ding and ren." These were the mnemonics given to me by my teacher. I have explained them for your benefit. Those who have heard these explanations should consider themselves fortunate and should take these teachings seriously.

26

The Difference between Lead and Mercury

The spirit within the mind is called the original nature of mercury. The generative essence in the mind is called the fluid of mercury. The original nature of mercury is gathered in the Yellow Pavilion, and the fluid of mercury is accumulated in the Purple Pavilion. They are the mercuric dragon and the true mercury. Together they are referred to as the internal pill, the yin pill, and the post-celestial half-pound son.

The vapor in the body is the essence of lead. The generative energy in the body is the splendor of lead. The essence of lead is obtained from the palace of kan, and the splendor of lead is gathered in the house of dui. They are called the lead tiger and the true lead. Together they are referred to as the external pill, the yang pill, and the pre-celestial eight-ounce mother.

27

Discussion on the Cauldron

In internal alchemy, qian and kun make up the cauldron, and kan and li are the medicine. If you use kan to replenish li, metal will return to its source. Kun is empty in nature (as depicted by the three broken lines of its trigram) and resides in the extreme yin of earth. Within kun is the seed of the first yang ready to be born. Qian is filled by nature (as depicted by the three solid lines of its trigram) and resides in the extreme yang of the sky. Within qian is the seed of the first yin ready to emerge. In accordance with the natural principles of the universe, that which is solid cannot receive, but that which is empty can. Thus, the emptiness of kun is used to enclose the solid. It is the solidity of yang that must fall into the embrace of emptiness. This is how the method of paired practice works.

When metal returns to its source, it can distinguish the difference between aged and fresh medicine. The pre-celestial qian hides in the house of kun. In this state, yang is enclosed by yin. Like the hidden water of kan, its workings are secret. Until metal emerges in the water, like the western moon descending at dui, it cannot be used. The medicine should be collected at the moment metal emerges, because at this time the energy is pristine and formless. To gather it at dui when the metal emerges in water is equivalent to gathering it at kan. That which is born in dui is now equivalent to that which is born in kan. If the light of the generative essence of the father of qian is absent, the great medicine cannot emerge. Allow qian to be the host and let yourself be the guest. If he wants to float, then you should sink. The rising and falling of host and guest take place within the cauldron, and the key to setting up the cauldron is emptiness.

Immortal Tao said, "There is actually nothing within the cauldron." What does he mean? At age fourteen, the light of the generative essence of father qian is felt, as yang energy begins to stir. At this time, there is nothing in the qian cauldron. During the process of gathering, the yang lead of the kun mother must be absorbed into the empty cauldron. Otherwise, the golden pill cannot materialize. What we call the cauldron is a vessel that has the capacity to hold and store. These are the most subtle teachings of paired practice. Make sure you understand them well.

28

Qian, Kun, Kan, Li

Generally, qian and kun are considered pre-celestial, and kan and li are considered post-celestial in nature. However, it is said that post-celestial kan and li are hidden within pre-celestial qian and kun, and pre-celestial qian and kun are hidden within post-celestial kan and li. What does this mean?

Qian and kun are considered pre-celestial because they are manifestations of primordial yang, the state of the body before the onset of puberty. Internally, the virgin body embodies the quality of qian where yang is secured within. Externally, it has the quality of kun because yin is embodied in its softness. This is why qian and kun are regarded as pre-celestial in nature. Kan and li are considered post-celestial because they are manifested in our bodies after the onset of puberty, a state in which primordial yang has leaked out. When kun embraces qian, kan arises, and when qian embraces kun, li emerges. This is why kan and li are regarded as post-celestial in nature.

Strictly speaking, qian, kun, kan, and li are all present in pre-celestial existence. This is why qian and kun are used to create the cauldron and kan and li are used as medicines. The four are also present in post-celestial existence. This is why we use the workings of kan and li to recover the original structure of qian and kun.

Pre-celestial kan and li are used in the post-celestial process of refining the self because this process requires extracting kan to replenish li. When this is effected, the jade elixir can be returned to the dantien. Pre-celestial kan and li are also used in the process of recovering the primordial essences because this process requires transforming kan into li. When this is effected, the golden elixir can be produced and returned to the dantien. Both the pre- and post-celestial processes of attaining kan are referred to as pre-celestial procedures. The only difference between the two is whether we use that which comes from the other or plant and harvest it within ourselves.

My belief is that pre-celestial qian and kun are medicines from the primordial celestial domain, and post-celestial kan and li are medicines from the primordial human domain. If you are fortunate to receive the teachings while you still possess a virgin body, you can simply hold on to qian and kun in their pre-celestial state and attain the Tao. However, if your body has fallen into post-celestial existence, then qian and kun can only be used as components to build the cauldron.

29

The Subtle Method of Gathering and Refining

By gathering, we mean collecting the yang lead from the other to refine the vapor of the seed of the pearl within. The yang lead is the soul of the earth hidden in the extreme yin. Obtained during the process of refining the body, it can be used to tame the mercury and transform it into cinnabar grains. *Understanding Reality* says: "Use the soul of the earth to capture the cinnabar grains of mercury. If only people knew how to gather and refine this treasure!"

What do we mean by gathering? Gathering is the act of not-gathering. What do we mean by refining? Refining is the process of not-refining. What do we mean by not-gathering? It means stilling the tiger and keeping the dragon within. It also means holding on to the female and not focusing on the male. On the first day of the lunar month, vapor begins to rise. Following the movement of the vapor, the spirit rises as well, and both are brought into the cauldron. All this occurs naturally. This is why we say that gathering is the act of not-gathering. What do we mean by not-refining? It refers to the presence of the other in my home. When medicine meets fire, yin will dissolve and yang will strengthen. When yang is accumulated in the cauldron, it will circulate naturally. This is why we say that the process of refining is not-refining. However, during the times of gathering and refining, you must focus the spirit. The breath must be regulated and the spirit must be focused before gathering and refining can occur. When gathering and refining are complete, the generative energy will be transmuted into vapor. When sufficient vapor has accumulated inside the body, the belly will be solid and full, and the internal pill will materialize.

30

The Waterwheel

The waterwheel is the key to circulating the medicine. The work of the waterwheel is not a matter of imagination or conscious intention. It is the flow and ebb of vapor in the hours of zi and wu, the closing and opening of the yin and yang orifices, and the internal ascent and descent of fire.

When the foundation of the pill is complete, the golden cauldron will be filled. When the internal breath is regulated, the spirit will be focused internally. When the spirit is focused, spirit and breath will be synchronized, and wind and fire will copulate. Suddenly, the numinous sprout will eject its light and the gears of the mechanism will move. When this occurs, it is time to engage the waterwheel and start the process of refining. The movement of the wheel begins at the bottom of its circuit. Next, the movement travels through the du meridian, moving upward in reverse to the Celestial Valley cavity. Finally, the movement will enter the Central Palace. This is what happens when you attain the medicine. Few people understand the nature of the waterwheel. They think that they can get the wheel to move by imagining its movement. If you believe that you can get the wheel to move by thinking about movement, you are deceiving yourself, because nothing will happen.

I will now explain the nature of the waterwheel to you. The subtlety of the wheel lies in focusing the intention internally while allowing the spirit to fly outside. Many doubt the validity of this statement. They argue that the true spirit is the true intention, and as one single entity, how can these two be separated? Is the master inside or outside? How can there be two subordinates? This kind of questioning is understandable. I will now clarify this ambiguity.

First, you must understand that when the spirit is focused within, it should be kept still. Do not try to move the spirit. That which moves is the true intention. This is the key to engaging the Microcosmic Orbit. If you want the circulation to run smoothly outside, then it must be directed from the inside, and this internal director must be the true intention. The principle is similar to our relationship to our shadow. When we stand in front of a light, we cast a shadow on the wall. When we move, the shadow will move. Let me illustrate again with the example of speech. When we want to speak, sounds are produced. Thus, the wish to say something is followed by speech. The wish to speak is the director of the voice, and the body is the director of the shadow. Similarly, intention is the director of the movement of the waterwheel. We cannot see or hear this internal director, so for convenience, we call it intention.

The spirit is circulated outside. It is two and yet one. If there is internal circulation, there will also be external circulation. If you do not try to control the circulation, the two (spirit and intention) will naturally come to know each other. Why? The true intention resides in the center inside. If you regulate the breath, the internal and external circulations will be synchronized. When the true intention moves, you will feel something thrusting through the gates and moving to the top of the head. You will be only vaguely aware of the presence of the spirit, but you will feel the movement of intention clearly. When the spirit circulates, it becomes the true intention; when still, it remains as the spirit. Immortal Wu said, "When you feel spirit and intention becoming aware of each other, you will understand what this is all about." I can't tell you how spirit and intention can become two and yet are one, and how the internal and external circulations can be synchronized, because this knowledge is intuitive and not conscious. I can only tell you that you need to tame the intention and regulate the movement of breath internally. The movement of vapor is not forced, and the wind that drives its movement occurs without conscious knowledge or intervention. You will feel the presence of intention, but you will also feel the spirit floating out there somewhere. When I reach this state, I don't even know whether spirit and intention are one or separate. I only feel that internally I have focused this entity within my home, and externally I am directing it up to the Celestial Gate *(tienmen)* cavity. I have no idea of how spirit and intention can become aware of each other. This is indeed the subtlest of all subtleties. The internal universe is a kaleidoscope of feelings of the immortal floating and wandering in the silver stream, welcoming the jade petals falling, and returning leisurely to the Yellow Pavilion. The wheel is running smoothly and the spirit is flowing free in exaltation. Daily it circulates; every morning it swirls back and forth. Penetrating the hundred joints, it moistens the three palaces. When you reach this stage, the medicine will not leak out and the true vapor will be plentiful.

Many practitioners don't understand the workings of the waterwheel. If you try to engage the wheel by thinking about it or imagining its movement, you'll only be wasting your time and effort. I hope that from this explanation of the nature of the wheel, students can find a legitimate teacher and learn the techniques properly.

31

The True Mind

The true spirit, true vapor, and true generative essence must be attained before any internal transformation can occur. If you don't have the true mind, you won't be able to attain the true generative essence, true vapor, and true spirit. By true mind, we mean the state of mind before the emergence of knowledge and thought, before the arousal of sexual desire, and before the contamination of the sprouts. The key to spiritual cultivation lies in entering and maintaining stillness. Practitioners who are not adept in the techniques of refining the body must first cultivate stillness. Otherwise, they cannot progress. They must quiet the mind whenever they can. This is akin to the military strategy "advance when the opportunity arises and attack before the opposition has prepared its defense." When you feel a spark of clarity in your mind, you should lock the three treasures within immediately. Focus the spirit and regulate the breath. Let no thoughts inside reach outside, and let no objects from the external world enter your thoughts. Seize the time when desire and thoughts have not yet emerged. Cultivate stillness, and you will obtain results. While the knowing mind is inactive, catch a glimpse of the true mind. While the vapor is not disturbed by emotions, take the opportunity to nourish the true vapor. Before sexual desire is aroused, start to accumulate the true generative essence. Focus your mind on absolute emptiness, hold on to stillness, and you will be able to enter the Mysterious Gate. This is the first principle of cultivating body and mind.

The workings of the true mind are subtle. If you are anxious over mundane matters, or are concerned with socializing and entertaining, the mind will become active. When you sense that worldly and materialistic things are taking over your thoughts, you should tame the mind. When the mind wanders, all kinds of thoughts will arise. It is best if you can stop these thoughts immediately. However, even after you empty the mind, stray thoughts can return after a while, growing and increasing in strength. When this happens, you must act as if you are faced with a great enemy. Close your eyes and fight the greatest battle you've ever known. Drive the opposition from the battlefield, and the active mind will be defeated.

Beginning practitioners have not seen through the illusions of the mundane world. Thus, they can't forget everything in the midst of the swirling dust, and they don't intuitively understand the meaning of emptiness. This is because, unlike adepts, they have not attained the highest wisdom. Even to begin to have an understanding of original nature is no small achievement. Beginning practitioners must seek the true mind and enter the gate of stillness even if they have started to refine the body. My advice to all practitioners is this: Once you have encountered the true mind, do not lose it.

The true mind can be attained when you are relaxed, be it in the quiet of the night or during the busy hours of the day. It is up to you to attain and keep it. Although it is called the true mind, this name is given for convenience. You won't find this term in the old internal alchemical texts. The name "true mind" came about only when practitioners began to discuss this state of mind more openly. The important thing is that you should always hold on to the true mind and embrace it daily. Every day and every hour, you should not lose track of the true mind. In time, its occasional emergence will become constant, and you will attain pure stillness. The practice of holding on to stillness continues to the higher levels of cultivation, so don't think that once you have attained it, the work is finished. To realize the one spark of clarity in the mind requires a lot of work. Therefore, you should treasure this stillness and clarity and appreciate the precious moment when the true mind emerges.

32

The Mind and the Spirit

The mind is the ruler of the body, and spirit is the highest of the three medicines. Are mind and spirit one entity or two? This needs to be explained. Laozi said, "The spirit tends toward stillness but is distracted by the mind." The sage Lu Qianxui said, "Regulating the breath begins with regulating the mind, and focusing the spirit begins with regulating the breath." This is the advice given by the sages and immortals on attaining enlightenment and merging with the Tao.

If you are serious about cultivating the Tao, you must banish all thoughts and return to stillness. Whether walking, standing, sitting, or sleeping, you must hold on to stillness. The mind that thinks is the wayward mind; the mind that has no thoughts is the true mind. If you can minimize your thoughts and stop them before they arise, then you will be able to focus your mind and strengthen the foundation for entering stillness. The sages say, "If you know how to stop thinking, you will be still." If you are still, you can attain quietude. When the mind is quiet, it will be easy to regulate the breath. The quieter the mind, the softer the breath will be. If the breath is regulated, the spirit will return to its rightful home and be focused within the cavity of the vapor.

The mind is sometimes referred to as the spirit. When mind is active, thoughts arise. When it is quiet, it can be tamed. When the mind is still, it will return to the chamber of the spirit where it will become the spirit. The spirit is none other than a mind without knowledge and thought. In nonaction, the mind becomes the spirit, and as spirit, it can do everything and be anything. It is for this reason that we consider spirit the highest of the three medicines.

To focus the spirit, we must synchronize its movement with the breath. Do not make the spirit control the breath, and do not force it to move the breath. When the spirit chases after the breath, it will dissipate. When the spirit forces the breath to move, it will be shaken. If you let the breath move naturally, the spirit will be focused. When you feel the first stirring of movement in absolute stillness, it is a sign that the spirit is coming into contact with vapor, and vapor is emerging from the undifferentiated chaos. In absolute stillness, spirit is quiet. In movement, it travels without obstruction. Those who cultivate the Tao should know this well.

33

Joint Functions of Spirit and Breath

⁓

Spirit is fire and breath is wind. If you want to understand the subtle workings of wind and fire, you must calm the spirit and regulate the breath. The spirit needs to be still before it can embody the light, and the breath must be regulated before it can receive the true vapor. While the spirit should be stilled, it must also be able to move and follow the breath naturally. We can compare this to stoking a fire in a furnace. When we pump the bellows, air is turned into wind, and with each pumping, the fire gets hotter. When the fire is hot, it can transform metal. In the tempering of metal, it is the wind that fans the fire, not the fire that fans the wind.

There is one important key to this process. If you want to pump the air in bursts, you must position the bellows close to the furnace, so that there is little time between when air is being pushed in and when it is sucked through the bellows. Only then can the fire of the furnace turn blue and burn hot. The activities of focusing the spirit and gathering the vapor are similar to tempering metal. The breath needs to be directed at kan; this means that you must position the bellows close to the furnace in order to help the wind fan the fire. When the fire in the furnace is ignited and the bright flames are dancing about, the spirit will become vapor. This vapor is the medicine. When the fire tempers the iron, the iron will become one with the fire. This is what the sage Qingguan meant when he said that the fire is the medicine and the medicine is the fire. When fire and medicine interact and merge, the golden pill will materialize. However, if the breath is not directed deep inside but instead is routed through the throat, mouth, or nostrils, nothing will happen: It is equivalent to positioning the bellows far from the furnace. We can only pity those who make this terrible mistake.

34

Further Discussion on Spirit and Breath

When the breath is still, spirit will return to its rightful place. Thus, the key to focusing the spirit lies in regulating the breath. When the spirit is still, the breath will be slow and calm. The key to regulating the breath, therefore, lies in focusing the spirit. The spirit must enter the void before the internal breath can emerge. When the internal breath emerges, the breath will attach itself to the spirit and remain calm. When the breath is calm, the spirit will stay in the embrace of the breath and not stray. When both spirit and breath are still, they are in a state beyond existence and nonexistence. In this state, we won't know whether spirit is breath or breath is spirit. When you sense that there is no differentiation between breath and spirit, you should stoke the fire. When wind is applied to fire, the flames are fanned. When fire receives wind, it will become hot. Stoke the fire until wind and fire are merged and locked together. When practice is perfect, the results attained cannot be described in words.

35

The Subtle Workings of Vapor and Breath

Immortal Cao Yuan said, "The root of life comes from the true breath." What do we mean by this?

In regulating the breath, we synchronize the post-celestial breath with the pre-celestial breath. Pre-celestial breath is the true vapor within the body. This true vapor can be moved by the breath. When breath is regulated, it will come and go smoothly and gently. With time and practice, we won't know whether it is breath or vapor that is moving. When the breath moves, vapor will also move. When the two can no longer be differentiated, then breath and vapor will have become one. This is why it is said that the true breath is ephemeral and subtle, and that breath is always present in vapor. The true breath is like a bellows. When the true breath moves, the true vapor will emerge. The true vapor originates from the root of life. It is that which allows us to recover, nourish, and preserve life. This is the true function of the true breath.

36

The Subtle Workings of Spirit and Intention

The spirit works best when it is focused. The *Triplex Unity* describes this state as "abiding in the stillness of the void and letting the light reflect back into the body." Spirit is not equivalent to intention. However, we need to use the true intention to reflect the light into the Mysterious Gate. I have heard the sage Zhongxui describe the true intuition as that which emerges in absolute stillness. Qianxui said, "In order to moisten the upper and lower halves, the primordial spirit must swirl around between them." The swirling of the primordial spirit is that which brings the true intention out of the primordial spirit. Do not equate the primordial spirit with the true intention. The two are different in both structure and function. The spirit is ephemeral and is rooted in nonaction; it is that which directs all things in stillness. Intention is orderly and is grounded in organized activity; it is always straightforward and open. This is why the spirit is the lord of the pill and intention is the minister. It is also why we say that spirit and intention differ in both structure and function. Because they are two separate entities, they have separate functions. However, because they originate from the same source, they embody the same substance.

If you want to strengthen the true intention, you must nourish the primordial vapor. The true intention is born from absolute stillness and can help us attain the Tao. For the Taoists, the true intention is that which is "always constant and still"; for the Confucians, it is "action that is made possible by staying focused"; and for the Buddhists, it is "wisdom born from stillness."

37

Further Discussion on Spirit and Intention

When you lower your eyelids and begin to meditate, there is no need for spirit and intention to separate. Spirit and intention separate only when movement and stillness begin to follow each other in cycles. Focus the spirit in the Central Palace, but do not replace it with intention. When you have reached absolute emptiness, you should hold on to stillness. When the cycle of movement and stillness starts, you should start the furnace. It is possible that, in this stage, you can focus the spirit in the Central Palace. However, do not replace it with intention. The process of focusing the spirit is similar to that of capturing the lead and taming the mercury: You become the ruler of the celestial movement and act as the go-between. Why? Spirit and intention function differently. The spirit works through nonaction, and intention works through action. It is in nonaction that the spirit can accomplish everything. Intention, on the other hand, works in the realm of action and reaction. The spirit is the ruler of the intention, and intention acknowledges spirit to be its true primal origin. The spirit tends toward stillness and does not move. Intention, on the other hand, moves. In its movement, intention directs spirit; thus intention is spirit set in motion. Spirit must work together with intention in order for true intuition to emerge. If you want to nourish the primordial spirit, you must extinguish all thoughts. Only then can the spirit work in nonaction and attain everything.

The sage Shangyang, commenting on the *Triplex Unity,* said, "The realized being hides in the great depth and uses nonthinking to respond to everything." Therefore, you too should float and wander within the great center. Use nonthoughts to direct things, and let inhalation and exhalation embrace and nourish each other. Use the state of no-thought to attain this state of being. When the three natures meet, let nonthinking guide you to enter and use it. If you want to circulate the true intention, you must first refine the body. Only then can you respond with the appropriate action. Qianxui said, "Refine the celestial stem ji; seek lead, and use ji to welcome it. When you have obtained the lead, use ji to escort it into the cauldron. In bathing and steaming, use ji to hold it still. When incubating and nourishing, use ji to complete it." The subtle workings of the ji of earth do not stop here. Spirit and intention are integral to the generation and completion of the golden pill. The two cannot be isolated. As for their other uses, this will vary among people. I have merely told you some of the prevailing ideas concerning the relationship of spirit and intention.

38

Being a Warrior and Lasting Forever

The ancient sages said, "The great ones planted their virtue, saw their works come to fruition, and then imparted their teachings. In this way, their legacies last forever." That which lasts forever is a part of the Tao, and since the deeds of the sages support the way of the Tao, they are constant and indestructible. The virtue of compassion forms the foundation of the Tao; the virtues of softness and yielding are the functions of the Tao; the virtue of saving the world forms the structure of the Tao; and the method of self-cultivation is the Tao applied to everyday life. Spoken words are used to communicate the principle, and written words are used to record the teachings of the Tao. In speaking and writing about the Tao, the sage is as fearless as a warrior, and being fearless, his legacy lasts forever. To be mundane is to be perishable; to be a sage is to be timeless.

The warrior lasts forever because she does not fight with anyone and yet fights with all adversaries. In not fighting, she softens motivation and tames hardness, and puts herself last in order to return to the beginning. In fighting adversaries, he is the fearless warrior and the indefatigable fighter. Embodying the steadfastness of the hero and the power of the conqueror, he is not involved in the petty battle of the common person but fights the battles for countless generations to come. Confucius said, "The virtuous person is not a common general. The common general is afraid that if he does not fight, he would be considered a coward." Other

Confucian sages have said that a peaceful spirit clear as night is no different from the mind of the sage. If you attain this state of peacefulness, you'll be like Confucius and Yanzi. The Buddhists say that if you embody virtue in stillness, you will be no different from the Buddha. The Taoists say that it is from earth and not sky that immortals Zhongli and Lu come. To be a warrior of the Tao means to surpass those who have lived before us. Let all practitioners become warriors of the Tao. Like sages past and present, be fearless in propagating the way of the Tao.

39

Retreating from the World after Serving the World

The *Tao Te Ching* says: "To retreat from the world after you have served it is the natural way of heaven." The way of humanity should follow the way of heaven, and the way of cultivating the self should be grounded in the way of humanity. Creation is the great accomplishment of the celestial way. However, after creation, when things grow and mature following their natural course, heaven hibernates and no longer interferes in the ways of humankind. Following the same principle, we humans need to exercise virtue and contribute to the well-being of all. However, when our work is finished, we should have the courage and wisdom to retire and hide. This is why the sage and the hero can wander leisurely with immortals like Chisunzi.

As part of humankind, it is natural for us to be filial to our parents and serve our community and the world. However, after our parents have left, after our children have grown and gone, and after we've served the world, it's time for us to retire and devote ourselves to spiritual cultivation. The sage abides in stillness and emptiness and understands what it means to achieve by not achieving. Elusive and ephemeral, he delights in becoming synonymous with anonymity. When the sacred fetus is conceived and he is ready to return to the source, he retreats into the cavity of the primal beginning, embraces the One, and returns to the void. This is the way of the sage.

40

The Joint Taoist, Buddhist, and Confucian Paths of Spiritual Cultivation

The dual cultivation of mind and body forms the foundation of Taoist, Buddhist, and Confucian spiritual training. Some say that the Buddhists cultivate mind exclusively, the Taoists cultivate body exclusively, and the Confucians are concerned only with building harmonious social relationships. They think that these paths are incompatible because they don't understand the deep teachings of these three wisdom traditions.

As far as I know, while the Buddhists focus on cultivating mind (and recovering original nature), they have secret teachings on cultivating the body. They emphasize cultivating the mind because they believe that it is best for their followers to begin spiritual development by returning to the original mind and letting original nature shine. The Taoists emphasize cultivating the body, but cultivating original mind is essential to their teachings. They focus on cultivating the body because they believe that it is by recovering the original body that the practitioner can build a strong foundation for the root of life and eventually attain original mind.

If you attain the highest level of cultivating the mind but neglect the body, you won't be able to keep original mind for long. If you can't keep the original mind, your cultivation will come to nothing and you won't be able to transcend samsara. If you manage to reach the highest level of cultivating the body but neglect to cultivate the mind, then the true energy of life cannot be held in the body for long. If you can't preserve the body, how can you penetrate the secrets of the celestial, terrestrial, and human realms?

The Buddhists have secret teachings on cultivating mind to attain life, entering the western realm, and merging with the void. On the other hand, the Taoists have teachings on how to cultivate the body to attain nirvana and be liberated from suffering in samsara. Buddhism and Taoism both have methods of single and paired cultivation as well as techniques of spirit travel. The Buddhists, after reaching the state of Chan stillness, can send the spirit out of the body through the top of the head. They have techniques that enable yin and yang to copulate and male and female energies to interact. The Taoists also have techniques that reach the same goals. Consider this statement made by Lu Dongbin: "To cultivate the mind exclusively at the expense of neglecting the body is the first mistake of spiritual practice." And Zhang Ziyang said, "If you understand original nature, you won't throw away your life energy. And, if you practice the paired method of cultivation, you'll be able to attain the great medicine, prevent the essence of life from dissipating, and become a realized being."

Attaining a deep state of absolute stillness, emptying the five senses, completing the pill and accomplishing its great return (to the dantien), facing the wall for nine years, attaining omniscience at age sixty, and becoming one with original nature at age seventy—these practices all require cultivating both body and mind. Only when you have completed these stages of spiritual development can you enter the ultimate realm and merge with the void. Both the Buddhists and Taoists agree on this.

Bodhidharma once said, "The three families—Buddhism, Taoism, and Confucianism—are built on the same foundations. Don't think that mind and body are unrelated." Body and mind must both be cultivated jointly, and understanding the natures of qian and kun is the key to everything.

If you understand the teachings of the three paths—Confucianism, Buddhism, and Taoism—you'll know that they are not contradictory. They may use different techniques, but they all lead to the same goal. A great Taoist teacher once said, "Let me tell you about the three paths. When separate, they are three; when combined, they are one." If the Tao does not manifest itself through differentiation, the power of creation and transformation cannot be realized. If after differentiation the aspects of the Tao cannot be merged again, then they cannot return to the one source. Thus, the three paths build three types of foundations. Buddhism specializes in recovering the original mind; Taoism specializes in building the foundation of life; and Confucianism focuses on building a harmonious society. But, without original nature and original life, how can a harmonious society be created? Many practitioners of these three paths don't understand the essence of the teachings. They believe that Confucianism, Buddhism, and Taoism are contrary paths. They inflate the differences and misrepresent the teachings. They voice their opinions, criticize each other, and stir up conflicts among the Buddhist, Taoist, and Confucian communities. The three spiritual traditions have spawned many illegitimate children who have nothing but negative opinions of each other. These children don't understand that the three different paths lead to the same goal. Unable to see beyond their own perspective, they are convinced that a path different from theirs must be false. Such people need to look into the source of the traditions before they criticize or even talk about other spiritual paths.

In my opinion, there are three approaches but one source and one goal. In one path, life is recovered by cultivating original nature; in the second path, original nature is attained by cultivating life; and in the third, life and original mind are cultivated through building a harmonious society. Although these are three distinct approaches, they all lead to the one undifferentiated source. Ponder this saying: "When naughty children turn off the lights, people will attack their own family."

Secret Teachings on the Three Wheels

(SANJUBIZHI)

Introduction

The three wheels refer to the three waterwheels. The first wheel circulates vapor. It is called the Microcosmic Orbit and is involved in the application of fire in the hours of zi and wu. The second wheel circulates generative energy. It is known as the waterwheel of the jade elixir and is used to move water for purposes of incubating and nourishing the sacred fetus. The third wheel circulates both generative energy and vapor. It is called the Macrocosmic Orbit and is involved in moving the pre-celestial metal of mercury. This wheel is responsible for returning the numeric seven and the numeric nine to the dantien to complete the great pill. The movement of the three wheels is driven by true spirit and true intention. If you understand the secret of the three wheels, the generative, vital, and spirit energies within you will be strong and wholesome, and you will be able to attain human, terrestrial, and celestial immortality.

I

The First Waterwheel

The circulation of vapor is necessary for opening the gates, building the foundation, attaining the medicine, and realizing the pill. The process begins with nourishing the true breath in stillness and emptiness. Tame the mind and regulate the breath by closing the eyes and keeping the spirit focused within. When you attain absolute stillness, a spark of clarity will emerge. Let go of everything until there is no differentiation between yourself and the external world. Be still and return to the root, like things lying dormant in winter. Oblivious to day and night, with no duality of knowing and not knowing, let the mind be at rest. It is in this state of not thinking and not knowing that the one yang will emerge. When the one yang stirs, you will feel the presence of smoke, yet there is no smoke. You will feel vapor stirring, yet you are not sure whether there is something rising from the lower dantien to the heart. When you feel as if you've just awakened from a deep sleep, you will be in a state known as the "living hour of zi." At this time, you must start the first waterwheel immediately and keep it moving. If you delay, the formless vapor will take on form and be lost. This vapor is the lead of the celestial stem ren and is also known as the post-celestial yang fire. Since it emerges in zi, this is why we apply fire in the hour of zi.

What is meant by stoking the yang fire? It means taking the just-awakened mind and directing it down to the Raven Bridge (qiaoqiao) cavity, which is the cavity just below the area of the

Celestial Wheel *(tienji)*. As far as I know, this teaching has not been transmitted publicly. This mind is called the mind of the sky and the earth. Sometimes it is referred to as the subtle mind, the primordial spirit, the true intention, and the Mysterious Gate. Next, the intention associated with the subtle mind is directed down to the Tailbone cavity. Hold it there and do not let it wander. After a while, the true vapor will begin to heat up. Once heated, the vapor will rise from the two cavities at the tip of the tailbone through the lower spine up to the Jade Pillow *(yuzhen)* cavity and into the Mudball cavity. The immortals tell us that the cavity in the middle spine named Between the Shoulder Blades *(jiaji)* is linked to the top of the head, and that those who cultivate the Tao must walk this royal road of the spinal column. Many people don't know how to circulate vapor. They think that the key to circulating vapor is pressing the tongue against the palate to produce the sweet nectar there. This is pitiful. They make this mistake because they have no teacher to instruct them. You must know that during its circulation, the vapor must be directed through the throat. The *Yellow Pavilion Classic (Huangtingjing)* says: "Ingest the mysterious vapor to attain longevity." This vapor of yang fire is dark purple in color and is called the mysterious vapor. To ingest it, you must receive instructions orally from a teacher. Only then can you know how to direct it through the throat into the upper respiratory system. Otherwise, the vapor will go into the esophagus, and the foundation of the pill will never be built. The vapor must be channeled down the throat into the Mysterious Orifice *(xuanwei)* cavity, where it is transmuted into sweet nectar. The *Yellow Pavilion Classic* describes this process as "the Mysterious Orifice of the breath channel receiving the magical generative essence." The Mysterious Orifice cavity is also known as the Mysterious House *(xuanhu)* cavity or the Mysterious Closure *(xuanyong)* cavity. When vapor enters this cavity, it will be secured and locked within. Many people don't know the subtle workings of the vapor. They think that when the vapor reaches the Mudball cavity, it will automatically be transformed into the sacred water, which is to be swallowed like tea or soup. If you swallow this liquid, you will cough violently. This is because fluids have form and therefore cannot be routed through the respiratory system. It is why the *Yellow Pavilion Classic* says: "The clear vapor comes out and the subtle vapor goes in during the exchange. When this happens, you will be able to ascend to the celestial realm." What this means is that the pure clear vapor comes out of the dantien and the subtle vapor enters the Mysterious Orifice cavity. When the two exchange, the vapor will be transformed into water, which will moisten the heart palace. From there it will descend into the cavity of the void. Treasure the water, cultivate it, and it will become the foundation of the pill.

In time, the foundation of the pill will be strong and vapor will be plentiful. When you have entered absolute stillness, you will suddenly feel a substance emerge from the dantien, roaring like wind and thunder and shooting up like a comet. This is a sign that the pre-celestial medicine has emerged from its hiding place within the post-celestial. When this happens, you should start the first waterwheel to move the substance into the Mudball cavity, where it will be transformed into a fluid. Ingest it and it will become the jade elixir of the head of the pill. This is the beginning of the crystallization of the medicine. Once the medicine emerges, you must circulate it ceaselessly, so that its roots are planted deep. To find out more about the subtleties of nourishing the pill, please study the next chapter.

2

The Second Waterwheel

To refine body and original nature, we need to circulate generative energy, and this circulation requires extracting the lead from
kan to replenish the mercury in li. When you have mastered the
process of circulating the vapor as described in the previous chapter, you will attain the lesser medicine, thus strengthening the head
of the pill. Now you are ready to engage the inner breath. Sit in
natural stillness and focus on the dantien. At dawn, cultivate clarity
whether you are sitting or lying down. In time, the pill will coagulate into something soft like a cotton ball. Let it rise to the heart,
but always return it to the void. It is important to keep the pill in
its formless state; otherwise it will dissipate. This is what the teachers meant when they said, "When the spirit returns to dwell inside
the body, the vapor will return as well." Once you have attained
absolute stillness, you will feel something gushing out of the
dantien, swirling and bubbling like the waters of spring rain. At
this time you must engage the natural inner breath. Heat the water
and it will be transformed into steam. Let it flow down your inner
thighs to enter the Bubbling Spring cavity. When you feel a sensation in the Bubbling Spring, you must focus the spirit, let the regular breath sink into the belly, and direct the true breath to follow
it. The true breath is none other than the "heavy breath of the realized being." When all is quiet and still in the Bubbling Spring
cavity, you should turn your attention to the Tailbone cavity and
wait patiently. In the midst of stillness, a substance will emerge

suddenly from the Tailbone cavity: something like a ball of cotton, or a lump of bread dough, or thick molasses. At this time, you should stop regulating the internal breath and focus your intention to refine this substance. If you are successful, you will feel a rush of hot liquid rising up from the Tailbone cavity to the spinal column in the area of the pelvis. From there it will ascend the spine and enter the Mudball cavity. This process is referred to as "the Yellow River churning and the Cao River flowing in reverse." This is the second waterwheel in motion; it is what the *Great Cavern Classic (Dadongjing)* referred to as "grabbing hold of the generative energy and escorting it into the Mudball cavity." Immortal Lu Dongbin described this phenomenon as "carrying the generative energy into the Central Palace."

When the second waterwheel is engaged, the water will roar like a waterfall inside the Mudball cavity. After a while, the sound of water will disappear. This is a sign that the spirit is at rest within the cavity. To hold the spirit in the Mudball cavity, you should place your tongue on the palate, hold your breath, close your mouth, clench the jaws, place your palms against your buttocks, turn your head upward toward the ceiling, and wait for the golden elixir to accumulate in the mouth. When you can no longer hold the breath, direct the fluid into the respiratory channel through the twelve rungs of the ladder to moisten the Radiant Pool cavity. The exact location and function of the Radiant Pool cavity are not known widely. Some practitioners say that it is just below the palate; others say that it is the lower dantien. These opinions are all incorrect. The Radiant Pool cavity is located below the two nostrils. It is also known as the Upper Sea of Vapor *(shangqihai)*, and it is near the Mysterious Orifice cavity. Immortal Baiyuchan said, "The Radiant Pool is located in the Sea of Vapor." When fluid is plentiful in the Radiant Pool, it will flow down to the Crimson Palace. When the Crimson Palace is moistened, you will feel a coolness washing over the body. Simultaneously, you will feel openness and joy in your heart. As the fluid continues to descend to the Yellow Pavilion, the fires of the heart will be quenched and you will feel peaceful and harmonious. This is the process of extracting lead to replenish mercury, or subduing the tiger and taming the dragon. When the hexagrams "After Completion" (*jiji*: li below, kan above) and "Before Completion" (*weiji*: li above, kan below) cycle back and forth ceaselessly, the jade elixir is at work refining the body. The jade elixir, however, does not emerge every day. Usually, it emerges only after several rounds of circulating the vapor. If the jade elixir can be made to emerge reliably, the Yellow Pavilion will be in order, the skin and complexion will be bright and rosy, the heart will feel at ease, and the light of original nature will radiate. You will be able to be at one with the world and not be attached to it. Desires will come and go but will have no hold on you. Following the natural course of things, you will be able to live among the dust of the world and not be tainted by it. The true intention is now firm and sharp and honed like a sword. Naked and without attachments, bright and still, you are now merged with the void. If you want to find out more about the third waterwheel, study the next chapter.

3

The Third Waterwheel

The circulation of pre-celestial generative energy and vapor is re-ferred to by the internal alchemists as "mercury welcoming the lead," "feelings returning to original nature," and "the return of the numerics seven and nine to the dantien."

When you have perfected the practice of refining the body, when mercury has become numinous and can flow and ebb with ease, and when female and male interact harmoniously, you can begin the great alchemical work of returning the numeric seven to the dantien. First, take the refined mercury and inhale it as the in-ternal pill. Then, go into a quiet room, sit in stillness, and secure and store the internal pill in the empty cavern. The top half of the pill is analogous to qian, and the bottom half is analogous to kun. The part that is original nature belongs to existence, and the part that is life belongs to nothingness. Begin by letting existence enter noth-ingness. In a little while, something will emerge out of nothingness. This is the process of planting the generative seed of qian in the mother of kun. When kun's belly is filled, it becomes kan. Now the generative essence of the kun mother will resonate with the qian father. When this happens, qian must empty its heart to become li so that it can receive the essence of kun. When the transformations of qian and kun are complete, they will become the cauldron. The functions of li and kan can now be applied. These processes are set in motion when existence enters nothingness. Now the mind must abide in stillness and become dead to things in the world. Only then can the spirit be kept within.

The knowing mind can fall prey to fear or love. The spirit will be tested and tempted as numerous monsters and warriors appear as benevolent and malevolent beings. When the spirit is not affected by these illusions, the primordial spirit will be focused. When the primordial spirit is focused, a ray of the light of yang vapor will suddenly arise. At this time, you should eject the one spark of yin from the palace of qian to welcome the yang. This is known as "using mercury to welcome lead," "the copulation of the great kan and li," and "dissolving the barriers between the internal and external yin and yang." When the barriers are down, you should tell the sacred lady of the primal beginning to take the female sword to harvest the substance that will become the ingredients of the pill. This is the process of returning the numeric seven to the dantien.

When the ingredients of the pill are secure, spirit and vapor will be in harmony. The one yang will grow and the trigram dui will be born. The male of kan will become the dui of the female. The dui of the female is what the internal alchemists refer to as the first menstrual blood, or the gui of the celestial stem. The gathering of this blood is called "taking the feelings and returning them to original nature." In five thousand forty-eight days, the blood will return to the Yellow Pavilion, and you will be filled with the brilliant light of the full moon. As the golden water fills the body, the primal pre-celestial generative essence and vapor will be plentiful, healthy, and strong. When you reach this stage of practice, you should start the Great Waterwheel immediately. When the circulation of this waterwheel reaches the Mudball cavity, you will feel a sweet fluid sinking into the mouth. The drops of this liquid are as large as a bird's egg. Although it tastes sweet, the liquid is neither honey nor nectar but the golden fluid of the great pill that is produced by the return of the numeric nine to the dantien. Make sure you swallow this liquid. The return of the numeric nine is sometimes referred to as "lead falling into the embrace of mercury." When metal is coupled with wood, post-celestial existence will return to pre-celestial. The fetus will be conceived and introduced to its mother, and when the fetus is embraced by the mother, it will be nursed and nourished day and night. In time, as you gaze within, you will see the internal organs glow with a bright light, because the true One now resides in them. When the period of incubation is complete, the mother will give birth to the infant. Nourish the infant in stillness. Warm and hold it every hour. When it is mature, move it from the Numinous Valley *(lingu)* cavity to the Celestial Valley cavity, where it will exit and reenter naturally. Once the spirit-child is confident of leaving and returning to its corporeal shell, it can travel to the realm of immortality and be transformed into wondrous beings.

4

The Beginning Stages of Cultivating the Mind

The key to nourishing life lies in the true breath. The sage Cao Wenri said, "The root of life comes from the true breath."

You must begin your spiritual cultivation by quieting the mind, minimizing speech, and regulating the breath. When the inhalation and exhalation through the nostrils become soft, you should close your eyes and focus your gaze inward. Direct the spirit to below the kidneys toward the Yin Bridge vessel *(yinqiao).* (The Yin Bridge vessel runs down the inner side of the leg.) After a while, direct the breath up to the cavity of emptiness. Once the breath has reached the cavity of emptiness, you should allow the true breath to take over naturally. If the mind is too rigorous and strict, you should tame it with the scholar (slow) fire. If the mind is too cold and calculating, you should engage the warrior (fast) fire. The key to everything lies in the subtle functions of using the scholar and warrior fires to heat and refine.

Don't be attached to the internal breath and don't push it along, but do not neglect it either. In stillness, your mind must be as empty as the void. However, if you feel the breath moving while abiding in stillness, the void is no longer empty. In the transition between emptiness and nonemptiness and the void and not-void, stillness will become more still and clarity will become even clearer. At this time, vapor and breath must move together, and the spirit in the mind must remain still. Let go of everything and forget about self and other. This is what the sages meant by "penetrating the primal state of nondifferentiation." In this state of nondifferentiation, vapor will emerge, its existence felt only by the primal spirit. Now is the time to engage the true breath. When the true breath begins to move, you will feel a slight itch in the area of the heart. You should massage that area of the body immediately and direct the breath into the cavity of emptiness in the chest. With time, the root of life will be born, the vapor of yang will grow, and you will be able to open the gates and circulate the vapor.

Focusing the spirit and regulating the breath are also integral to the beginning stages of cultivating body and mind. To focus the spirit is to gather the already-cleared mind inside. Do not open your eyes if you have not cleared your mind. Coax and persuade the mind to return home. Wait until it is clear, calm, and open before you gather the vapor into the cavity. This process is called focusing the spirit. Sit in absolute emptiness, do not sway, and do not incline forward or backward. It is only in this state that the spirit can be focused and led into the void.

It is not difficult to regulate the breath. When mind and spirit are still, the breath will naturally be still. All you have to do is to hold on to the naturalness of the breath and direct the sacred light to shine downward. This is what the sages mean by "regulating the breath in the Yin Bridge vessel and preparing it to meet the breath of heart in the cavity of vapor." Immerse the spirit in vapor and focus it in stillness in the Sea of Vapor cavity. If you don't force spirit and vapor to interact, they will copulate naturally. If you don't force them to connect, they will connect naturally. This is what is meant by "letting the spirit of two bodies intertwine." Hold on to original nature and don't let it go astray. Keep the spirit within and don't let it become sleepy or lethargic. These are the keys to entering the state of nondifferentiation.

To focus the spirit, you need to focus the mind on the area below the navel. To bring the vapor to the area below the navel, you need to regulate the breath. When you feel that spirit and breath are merged, you must hold on to the natural state of stillness and clarity. This is what is meant by "not neglecting." To be naturally clear and still—this is what is meant by "not forcing things." Practice quietude and softness. The breath must be lively, but the mind must be still. This is called "initiating the activity of penetrating." Let the void be the hiding place of the mind, and let nondifferentiation be the home of the sacred breath. Practice purifying breath, vapor, and spirit several times a day. Suddenly, you will forget that spirit and vapor are two entities, and without realizing it, the one yang will be born.

5

Questions and Answers on the Methods of Cultivating Body and Mind

A student asked, "To expose the secrets of the three waterwheels is to reveal the subtle workings of heaven. Do you not fear retribution from the celestial powers?"

Li Hanxui replied, "I've never intended to go against the will of heaven. I only want to help people live a better life.

"Those who undertake spiritual cultivation must first rid themselves of the mundane human mind and seek the mind of the Tao. Slow the breath and look for the true breath. Only then can you still the spirit, gather the vapor, and enter the state of nondifferentiation. Your cultivation cannot progress unless you attain this state of mind. This is why few can practice my teachings.

"Entering nondifferentiation is the first challenge in cultivating body and mind. The one pre-celestial vapor emerges from nothingness. Before you can attain the true breath, you must attain true nondifferentiation. The early stages of cultivation are the most difficult, but if you can overcome the hardships, you will receive the most wonderful reward at the end. To practice my methods, you must let go of all attachments to the body. When I was a beginning practitioner learning the method of nondifferentiation in the celestial caverns, it took me seven or eight years before I got an inkling of the meaning of the teachings. Today, students are impatient for progress and want fast results. How can they even begin to enter the path of the Tao?"

Another student asked, "Teacher, some people criticize you for giving out your knowledge casually. They say that you are wasting your effort by teaching people who will never understand."

Li Hanxui replied, "I am not bothered by these criticisms. People criticize because they don't understand the greatness of the path of the Tao. To attain the great Tao, you must first clear and purify both body and mind, focus the spirit, and regulate the movement of the vapor. And, to do these things, you must let go of everything and enter the state of nondifferentiation. Only when you have reached this state can you attain the true results. Those who think about or imagine attaining results will accomplish nothing, and those who talk and criticize without practicing are hurting no one but themselves."

A student asked, "Teacher, can evil people learn the teachings of the Tao?"

Li Hanxui said, "You know the old saying: What you've done in the past is past; what you do now is what matters. Thus, if evil people turn away from evil and begin to do good deeds, they can transform hell into heaven and change the dark vapor into red aura. There are three qualities that a practitioner must have: diligence, sincerity, and perseverance. Not one of these can be neglected. Be diligent, be sincere, persevere, and you will obtain results. Confucius once said, 'If you do not persevere, you can't become a shaman or a healer.' The same applies to cultivating the Tao. People spend ten years or more studying the literature and the arts to become a scholar. Do you think that cultivating the mind and refining the vapor are easier than studying classical literature?

"What is sincerity? Sincerity is yin in nature. In Taoism, it is an integral part of the Great Ultimate (taiji). The Buddhists equate it with the mind of the Tathagata. Mencius said, 'Those who are truly sincere will act only when they are ready. Those who are insincere will act before they are ready.' Thus, when you compare action with nonaction, you will understand that sincerity is yin in nature. The Confucians value sincerity and consider it sacred. Sincerity is the key to slowing the breath because in stillness the great structure and great function of all things can be realized. Thus, sincerity is the key to entering stillness. If the mind is still, it will not go astray. Sincerity is the key to attaining stability. If the mind is stable, it cannot be moved. Sincerity is the key to holding on to the center. If the mind is held and centered, it will not be tempted. Sincerity is the key to entering the state of nondifferentiation. If you abide in nondifferentiation, you will be able to penetrate all mysteries.

"Diligence is the foundation of learning. Diligence is required to nourish the natural breath and calm the natural mind. When true diligence is present, the breath will be soft and enduring, and its use will never be exhausted.

"When you combat the monster of sleepiness and lethargy, you must exercise diligence and discipline. If you continue to meditate when your spirit is lethargic, you will misuse diligence. Those who are adept at refining mind and vapor are in a state of wakefulness even when sleeping and in a state of rest even when they are fully awake. When your practice is natural and smooth, spirit will strengthen and vapor will increase naturally. If you meditate in the middle of the night, you must fight the monster of sleepiness. The *Triplex Unity* states: 'Stay in the embrace and be intertwined during sleep; wait for existence and nonexistence to occur during waking.' If you know how to use this advice, you will naturally achieve a trancelike state but will also be truly awake."

A student asked, "Master Lu Qianxui once said that the technique of copulation is a great secret coming from the most high. Can you tell us more about it?"

Li Hanxui said, "Copulation is the foundation of the absolute yin and the root of nonduality. Only when you are in a state of nonduality can you copulate successfully. I advise people to first refine themselves in emptiness. When stillness becomes absolutely still and calmness becomes absolutely calm, there will be no self and other. Emptiness itself will be empty, and you will be able to enter the state of duality naturally. If you don't think about copulation, copulation will occur naturally. It is from the depths of absolute yin that the absolute yang is born.

"There are two kinds of copulation: pre-celestial and post-celestial copulation. In pre-celestial copulation, original nature is used to build life; in post-celestial copulation, spirit is merged with vapor. The text *Adding the Medicine* states: 'We work with original nature and life, not just spirit and vapor. In the home of water, there is only one kind of lead.' While there is only one undifferentiated substance in pre-celestial existence, there are three in the post-celestial existence. In one aspect they are generative essence, spirit, and true intention; in another they are vapor, spirit (original nature), and feelings. If you are able to cultivate body and mind in the pre-celestial domain, you will be able to attain the primal substance easily, and in attaining this substance, you will attain everything. However, if you need to work through post-celestial existence, you'll need to cultivate the true yang through copulation.

"Within the mundane human body, the five viscera have fixed locations and cannot be moved around. However, in Taoist internal alchemy, qian, kun, kan, and li can exchange positions. Does this mean that the heart can physically be moved downward and the kidneys upward? No. What we mean is that the spirit and vapor in the heart and kidneys can move. The spirit in the heart can descend and the vapor of the kidneys can ascend. When spirit and vapor exchange places, the essences of the internal organs themselves—the formless qian and kun—will exchange places. When the exchange occurs, the one yang will be born in kun. Kun is then transformed into kan, and when the one yin is born in qian, qian will be transformed into li. When the female of li copulates with the male of kan, this is analogous to the female of dui in the west interacting with the male of zhen in the east. North and south are moved to west and east respectively, and water and fire become metal and wood. The feelings of metal and the original nature of wood are called the white tiger and green dragon respectively. When the dragon is attracted to the tiger, it is analogous to the new mother holding the infant. When the tiger is attracted to the dragon, it is analogous to the infant embracing the mother. Know that within life is original nature and within original nature is life. The two entities, life and original nature, are originally one. This is why Master Zhang Ziyang said, 'Zhen and dui are not concrete substances, and kan and li are not really north and south.' I hope you now understand the meaning of this statement.

"Although Confucians and Taoists both believe that nourishing the vapor is the key to attaining life, they have different methods and goals. The Confucians nourish the vapor of uprightness so that in the critical moment of life and death, they can make the right choice. In the past, many virtuous people gave their lives rather than compromise their integrity. If your goal is to uphold honor and integrity, you should cultivate this vapor. Mencius said, 'The vapor of uprightness is strong and tempered. Cultivate it in a straightforward way and you can save the world, for this vapor is born of all actions associated with honor.' The goal of the Taoists, however, is to preserve the true vapor. This is because they believe that there is no need to retreat or die when there is no honor left in society. You don't need to sacrifice yourself in order to keep your virtue. Observe the situation and respond naturally. Don't be attached to the idea that you must always play the role of the hero.

"Taoists begin their cultivation by nourishing the natural vapor. What is the natural vapor? The *Triplex Unity* tells us that this vapor is elusive and soft. Nourish it in a roundabout way and you will not come to harm. The natural vapor resides in the void. It is from this vapor that the generative essence is born. In contrast, the vapor that forms the foundation of returning the pill to the dantien is expansive and powerful. If you attain this vapor, you could, like the Confucians, have the strength to face danger or sacrifice yourself for the greater good. In the past, this kind of sacrifice has been used by Taoist adepts to shed the shell and liberate the spirit. The expansive vapor is capable of initiating wondrous and subtle things, and its transformations are endless. When Taoists shed their shell voluntarily, they can return to the earthly realm as spirit beings, appearing young and rigorous and often in the company of immortals. This is what the process of returning the pill to the dantien can accomplish.

"When you attain the Tao, bodies will emerge beyond your corporeal body, and when your time is over in the earthly realm, you can shed your shell and send the spirit into immortality. If you focus on cultivating the expansive vapor like the Confucians, you can attain the highest virtues and be remembered as a sage for eternity. In life you live fully, and in death your name is respected forever. The Confucian sages Zhangzi, who lived a long and full life, and Yanzi, who lived a short but full life, are examples.

"There are five obstacles that hinder you from the Tao. First, if you spend too much time trying different paths, you can never get to the higher stages of training. Second, if you choose the path of fame and temporal power, you will never attain the Tao. Third, if you start out diligent but become lazy with time, your practice will not progress. Fourth, if you are dogmatic and argumentative, or think that you know a lot, or challenge the teachers, you will never learn. Finally, if you have an inflexible mind, you will never be awakened even if you are constantly exposed to the teachings.

"Three levels of attainments are available to those who complete their cultivation. First, those with deep understanding of the Tao can become numinous beings and enter the celestial realm. Second, those who are sincere and motivated can become realized beings and live a long and healthy life on earth. Finally, those who delight in the Tao will become extraordinary people and live a meaningful and full life among humans."

Books by Eva Wong

Cultivating Stillness

Equanimity, good health, peace of mind, and long life are the goals of the ancient Taoist tradition known as "internal alchemy," of which *Cultivating Stillness* is a key text. Written between the second and fifth centuries, the book is attributed to T'ai Shang Lao-chun—the legendary figure more widely known as Lao-Tzu, author of the *Tao Te Ching*. The accompanying commentary, written in the nineteenth century by Shui-ch'ing Tzu, explains the alchemical symbolism of the text and the methods for cultivating internal stillness of body and mind. A principal part of the Taoist canon for many centuries, *Cultivating Stillness* is still the first book studied by Taoist initiates today.

Cultivating the Energy of Life

A classic Taoist manual on the circulation of internal energy by means of meditation and the inspiration for many techniques of Qigong. It is one of the few Taoist treatises to describe the landmarks of spiritual development and document the process of spiritual transformation from start to finish.

Feng-shui

The first complete, in-depth course in the traditional Chinese art of harmonious design for interiors, buildings, and sites—including instructions for making your own geomantic compass for feng-shui readings. Deeply rooted in Taoist and shamanic origins, feng-shui is not simply a list of directives for building auspicious structures or arranging interiors for good luck. It is the art of reading the patterns of the universe and living in harmony with the environment. With two hundred photos and diagrams.

Harmonizing Yin and Yang

To age with the sun and moon and be renewed by spring and summer, to conserve the seeds of growth in autumn and winter and to be nourished by the eternal breath of the Tao—these are the goals of the Taoist alchemists, the masters of the arts of health, longevity, and immortality. This book is a translation of a concise Taoist alchemical manual known as the *Dragon-Tiger Classic*, along with its two most important commentaries.

Holding Yin, Embracing Yang

The texts in this collection offer a clear view of the physical, mental, and spiritual methods of Taoist practice, showing why they are important and how these methods all can work together in the cultivation of mental peace, radiant health, and longevity. This collection will provide inspiration and the essential foundation necessary to begin Taoist practice under the guidance of a teacher.

Lieh-tzu

The *Lieh-tzu* is a collection of stories and philosophical musings of a sage of the same name who lived around the fourth century B.C.E. Lieh-tzu's teachings range from the origin and purpose of life, the Taoist view of reality, and the nature of enlightenment to the training of the body and mind, communication, and the importance of personal freedom.

A Master Course in Feng-shui

This fully illustrated, comprehensive workbook is designed primarily for homeowners, renters, architects, and business owners who want to put feng-shui to practical personal use.

Nourishing the Essence of Life

Eva Wong presents and explains three classic texts on understanding the Tao in the macrocosm of the universe and the microcosm of the body that provide an excellent overview of the three traditional levels of the Taoist teachings—Outer, Inner, and Secret.

Seven Taoist Masters

History and legend are interwoven in this folk novel that both entertains and instructs. Written by an unknown author, *Seven Taoist Masters* is the story of six men and one woman who overcome tremendous hardships on the journey to self-mastery.

The Shambhala Guide to Taoism

This guide to the spiritual landscape of Taoism not only introduces the important events in the history of Taoism, the sages who wrote the Taoist texts, and the various schools of Taoist thinking, but also gives the reader a feel for what it means to practice Taoism today.

Tales of the Dancing Dragon: Stories of the Tao

Arranged chronologically from prehistory through the early twentieth century, these stories introduce the schools in the Taoist lineages, and capture the defeats and victories of Taoism, its periods of decadence and decay, and its renewal, maturation, and spiritual triumph. Wong puts these stories into context, and shows that Taoism is a dynamic spiritual tradition, constantly changing—and being influenced by—history.

Tales of the Taoist Immortals

The stories in this book are of famous characters in Chinese history and myth: a hero's battle with the lords of evil, the founder of the Ming dynasty's treacherous betrayal of his friends, a young girl who saves her town by imitating rooster calls. The tales included here—which often have a moral behind them, are both entertaining and provocative.

Teachings of the Tao

Although the Tao cannot be described by words, words can allow us to catch a fleeting glimpse of that mysterious energy of the universe that is the source of life. The readings in this book are a beginner's entrée into the vast treasury of writings from the sacred Chinese tradition, consisting of original translations of excerpts from the Taoist canon.

Printed in the United States
by Baker & Taylor Publisher Services